Ghosts In The Darkness

Mysteries of the Temagami Wilderness

By

Timothy D

Temagami • Ontario • Canada

Copyright Page

Ghosts In The Darkness: Mysteries of the Temagami Wilderness© 2025 **Timothy D**

All rights reserved.No part of this book may be reproduced, stored in a retrieval system, or transmitted in any form or by any means—electronic, mechanical, photocopying, recording, or otherwise—without prior written permission from the author, except in the case of brief quotations used in reviews or critical articles.

This is a work of nonfiction.Witness accounts, researcher observations, and field reports used throughout this book are presented as provided by their sources.Some identifying details have been altered to respect privacy.

Cover Design: Timothy D**Interior Layout:** Timothy D

First Edition: 2025

ISBN: 978-1-0696715-2-3

TABLE OF CONTENTS

INTRO - THINGS THAT MOVED AT DUSK
CHAPTER 1 — THE TEMAGAMI ENIGMA
CHAPTER 2 — VOICES FROM THE PINES
CHAPTER 3 — THE WATCHERS OF THE DEEP WOODS
CHAPTER 4 — THE BIGFOOT PATTERN BEGINS
CHAPTER 5 — THE DRUMS, THE WHISTLES, THE SIGNALS
CHAPTER 6 — TRAILS THAT AREN'T THERE TOMORROW
CHAPTER 7 — TIME MISSING IN THE PINES
CHAPTER 8 — THE FOREST THAT REARRANGES ITSELF
CHAPTER 9 — VANISHINGS AND NEAR-MISSES
CHAPTER 10 — WINDLESS WHISPERS
CHAPTER 11 — THE SILENT ONES
CHAPTER 12 — TRACKS THAT SHOULD NOT EXIST
CHAPTER 13 — THE CABIN PACER
CHAPTER 14 — THE LAKE CREATURES
CHAPTER 15 — WOLVES THAT STAND TOO TALL
CHAPTER 16 — THE CLOAKED PRESENCES
CHAPTER 17 — THE NIGHT VISITORS
CHAPTER 18 — THE NIGHT THE FOREST TURNED AGAINST THEM
CHAPTER 19 — STRANGE LIGHTS OVER BLACKWATER LAKES
CHAPTER 20 — HAUNTED CAMPSITES OF OLD GROWTH TEMAGAMI
CHAPTER 21 — THE WOMAN ON THE WATER
CHAPTER 22 — PREDATORS THAT AREN'T BEARS
CHAPTER 23 — THE SCREAMING FOREST
CHAPTER 24 — THE DESOLATE PLACES
CHAPTER 25 — GIANTS OF TEMAGAMI
CHAPTER 26 — THE MIMICS
CHAPTER 27 — THE SHAPE OF THE UNKNOWN
CHAPTER 28 — TEMAGAMI'S INVISIBLE BOUNDARY
CHAPTER 29 — WHAT THE WITNESSES AGREE ON
CHAPTER 30 — THE CONSISTENCY OF FEAR
CHAPTER 31 — THE NIGHTS I COULD NOT EXPLAIN

APPENDIX A — ENCOUNTER CLASSIFICATION INDEX

APPENDIX B — CHRONOLOGICAL LIST OF REPORTS & CASE FILES
APPENDIX C — TEMAGAMI MYSTERY HISTORIC HOTSPOTS
APPENDIX D — TEMAGAMI CREATURE TYPES & BEHAVIORAL PATTERNS
APPENDIX E — ANOMALIES FOUND IN THE TEMAGAMI WILDERNESS
APPENDIX F — INDIGENOUS QUOTES & INTERPRETATIONS ON THE MYSTERIES OF TEMAGAMI
APPENDIX G — FIELD SAFETY & SURVIVAL GUIDELINES
APPENDIX H - TOP 10 MOST DISTURBING TEMAGAMI ENCOUNTERS
APPENDIX I — **ACTIVE** HOTSPOTS INDEX

ACKNOWLEDGEMENTS

INTRO: Thing That Moved at Dusk

Most stories worth telling don't begin with certainty. They begin with an unease that gnaws from the edges, something you notice only when the light is low and the forest has gone unnaturally still. Temagami is full of those moments. The old pines keep their own counsel, and the lakes say nothing at all—just lie there, black and reflective, waiting for someone to look a little too long into their surface.

The incident that pulled me deeper into the heart of this wilderness didn't happen on one of my longer expeditions or during a major investigation. It came from a paddler I'll call *R.*—a man who had spent more time in the Temagami backcountry than most people spend walking through their own neighbourhoods. A man who should have been immune to fear out there.

He wasn't.

It happened on a quiet autumn evening, the kind where the world cools fast and the shoreline turns purple in the last minutes of daylight. R. was paddling back toward his campsite on a small lake north of Morris Island. Calm water, no wind, no reason to think anything was out of place.

He said the first sign of trouble was the pacing—something moving step for step with his canoe along the treeline. Slow at first. Controlled. Almost thoughtful. He wasn't the type to panic. Bears, moose, wolves—he'd dealt with all of them. He told himself it was nothing.

Then the woods went silent.

Not "forest quiet." Not "end of day quiet." A deeper silence. A watching silence.

He stopped paddling. The canoe drifted. The surface of the lake smoothed into a long, amber mirror. He listened.

Nothing.

That's when he saw it—a figure stepping out from between the pines on the point to his left. He said it crouched low, like a shadow cast by a fire that wasn't there. Human-shaped, but too long in the limbs. Too still. Too deliberate.

He called out to it instinctively: *"If you're human, say something."*

It didn't.

Instead, the figure rose from its crouch and leaned forward slightly, as if scenting the air. And then came the sound—a low, wet, rolling murmur that didn't belong to any creature known to Temagami. Not a bear. Not a moose. Not a person.

The figure stepped backward into the darkness. No crack of branches. No scatter of leaves. It was simply *gone*.

R. paddled to the center of the lake and sat there until the sky turned black. He didn't build a fire that night. Didn't eat. Spent the whole night zipped inside his tent with trembling breath and cold hands. By first light, he packed up and left Temagami behind.

He hasn't returned since.

I've heard variations of that story before—too many times, from too many steady, seasoned outdoorsmen. R. wasn't dramatic. He wasn't gullible. He was a man who knew Temagami like an old friend, and that night Temagami showed him something he couldn't explain.

My Roots in This Wilderness

I've spent years researching in Temagami and the regions around it—years of boots on the ground, nights under canvas, and miles of shoreline paddled long after the last campers have gone home for the season. I live just an hour south of this place. Temagami isn't a distant legend to me. It's practically my backyard. I've walked its logging roads at dusk, listened to strange vocalizations echo across lakes, and felt the forest press in around the campsite when the fire dies too low. I've experienced "Bear"mageddon several times in Temagami, once on Gull Lake and another on Temagami access road during a TV Series I was working on for months in the summer of 2025, but that's another story.

I've investigated just about every type of strange encounter this region is known for—Bigfoot sightings, unexplained lights, vanishing footprints, shadow figures, murmuring voices. I've stood with fellow field researchers in the dark, our headlamps off, all of us holding the same question in our breath:

Did you hear that too?

Sometimes it's nothing.Sometimes it's something.Sometimes it's something you don't talk about until much later.

Temagami has a **vibe** at night—an electricity under the silence that's hard to explain unless you've felt it. A presence that sits just outside the firelight, patient and aware. You don't get that everywhere. Only in places that haven't been tamed. Places that still belong to themselves.

People often say, *"Well, I've been camping all my life and never seen anything strange."* I hear it constantly.

But that's not the proof they think it is.

The wilderness is vast. The encounters rare. The creatures—if that's what they are—do not wander up to your campfire and introduce themselves. Many who claim they've never seen or heard anything… weren't listening in the first place. They were talking. Cooking. Laughing. Busy. Distracted.

The forest does not show itself to those who aren't paying attention.

Some hikers and campers go their entire lives without noticing a thing beyond trees and trails. That doesn't mean the unknown isn't out there. It simply means it doesn't reveal itself to everyone.

Temagami, especially, does not give up its secrets easily.

Why This Book Exists

This book is not a collection of campfire stories. It's a record—of sightings, encounters, strange soundscapes, disappearances, and the moments when reality seems to fold just slightly at the edges.

Everything within these pages is rooted in real fieldwork, firsthand narratives, and evidence gathered over years. Not exaggerated. Not sensationalized. Presented as they came to me:honestly, unsettled, sometimes fragmented, always unforgettable.

There are things in Temagami that do not want to be found. Things that move when dusk hits the treeline, things that whisper at the edges of sleep, things that stare from the ridge when you think you're alone.

People like R. weren't imagining what they saw.Neither was I.Neither were the dozens of witnesses I've interviewed.

Temagami is watching. Temagami remembers. And every once in a while, Temagami lets something slip through—a glimpse, a sound, a presence—that reminds you just how ancient this land really is.

This book follows those moments. The cracks. The shadows. The encounters beyond the trail.

The Northern Unknown begins now.

CHAPTER 1 — THE TEMAGAMI ENIGMA

Why This Wilderness Holds More Sightings, Encounters, and Anomalies Than Anywhere Else in Ontario

1. A Land That Feels Older Than the Map

Ask anyone who has spent real time in the Temagami region—far from the campgrounds, far from the motorboats, far from the places where cell service still clings to the air—and they'll tell you the same thing:

There is something different about this place.

Not "different" in the poetic way people use when describing rugged landscapes. Different in a way that makes the hair rise on the back of your neck, even when the forest around you is quiet and there's no reason for it.

It's the silence between the pines. The cold breath off the blackwater lakes. The way shadows gather in the undergrowth long before the sun sets. And the way sound carries farther than it should, yet somehow reaches you softer than it ought to.

Temagami is a land that feels **inhabited**, even when you're the only human for miles.

And that's what this book begins with: **the uneasy truth that countless people have reported seeing—and hearing—things in these woods that defy explanation.**

Not a few isolated cases. Hundreds.

Across decades.

Across lakes. Across trails. Across seasons. Across generations.

Most people don't talk about it. But nearly everyone has a story.

2. The Unexplained Is Not New Here

One of the first things I learned while researching this book is that the unexplained in Temagami didn't begin with modern Bigfoot sightings or recent campers reporting mimicry or shadowy figures near their tents.

This land has been telling strange stories long before "cryptid" became a word anyone used.

Reliable Elders—people who know the terrain in ways maps can't capture—have spoken for years about:

- tall beings walking ridgelines at night
- voices calling from places no human could stand
- water creatures surfacing where no fish should be
- massive wolves following hunters silently
- lights drifting over black lakes with no source
- footsteps that stop at the edge of a cliff but leave no sign of a fall

They don't call these things monsters. They don't call them spirits. They don't call them aliens or entities.

They just say:

"There are others in the deep forest."

Not human. Not animal. Not named.

Just **others**.

And when you listen long enough to the people who live here, the feeling creeps in that the forest doesn't hide those others—it hosts them.

3. Why Temagami Has More Sightings Than Anywhere Else in Ontario

When you map out all known Bigfoot sightings, cryptid encounters, and unexplained wilderness events across Ontario, something strange becomes clear: **Temagami is the center of the storm.**

A perfect circle of anomalies.

Consider this:

- Northern Ontario is huge—larger than many countries.

- Yet **a concentrated cluster** of reports comes from the Temagami region.

- Sightings occur year-round, even in winter.

- Many come from unrelated, credible witnesses with no reason to lie.

- Patterns repeat across decades, even centuries.

Why here? Why this patch of wilderness?

When I started digging, several possibilities emerged:

1. Endless Old-Growth Forest

Temagami still holds some of Canada's most untouched old-growth stands. These forests are deep, layered, ancient—and provide cover for things that could easily avoid human detection.

2. A Complex Maze of Lakes and Ridges

Large bodies of blackwater, steep cliff faces, narrow channels, and hidden valleys form one of the most complex natural landscapes in Ontario. Anything intelligent and reclusive would thrive here.

3. Minimal Human Population

Outside a few towns and seasonal camps, the region is empty. Large creatures could roam for decades without crossing paths with a person.

4. Shared Boundaries With Vast Northern Wilderness

Temagami is not isolated—it is connected to thousands of square kilometers of unbroken land. Anything traveling east, west, north, or south has unlimited space.

5. A History of Unusual Activity

Witness accounts stretch back far before the modern era. The land has a reputation older than the country itself.

Together, these factors create the perfect conditions for something big, intelligent, and elusive to exist—and to avoid formal detection.

4. The Witnesses Who Changed Everything

Over the last several years, I've spoken with dozens of witnesses.Most were quiet about their experiences until I approached them privately.Not a single person wanted attention.Not one wanted to be published under their real name.

Here are a few examples that stuck with me:

A Veteran Fire Ranger

He spent twenty years patrolling Temagami's remote lakes. Quiet, practical, not prone to exaggeration.

He said:

"Something walked through my camp at night.Heavy. Two feet.Didn't speak. Didn't run.Just walked like it owned the place."

When I asked if it could have been a bear, he shook his head before I even finished the question.

"Bears don't walk like that."

A Retired Conservation Officer

Calm, steady, fully familiar with Temagami wildlife.

He described a dark figure crossing a granite ridge in three steps—steps far too long for any human.

His voice never changed when he told the story.He wasn't trying to convince me.He was reliving something.

A Group of University Researchers

They were conducting water sampling when they heard what they called "wood-knocking." Rhythmic. Deliberate.

When they knocked back—out of curiosity, not belief—they received a third knock in response.

They left the lake early.

A Young Canoe Trip Leader

She described hearing someone—or something—pacing outside her tent for nearly forty minutes at night.

Not circling. Just pacing.

Deliberate. Heavy. Measured.

The next morning, no tracks. Only flattened moss—large ovals, each one the size of a shovel head.

5. The Pattern Beneath All Stories

When you step back and look at everything at once—every sighting, every sound, every unsettling moment—something begins to emerge. A pattern modern science doesn't acknowledge, but one countless people have lived through.

That pattern has five key parts:

1. Height

Witnesses consistently describe figures between seven and nine feet tall.

2. Silence

These beings can move silently when they want to—even at massive size.

3. Intelligence

The encounters are not chaotic. They feel purposeful.

4. Territorial Behavior

Most encounters occur when humans inadvertently enter certain valleys, ridges, or shorelines.

5. Avoidance

Whatever is out there does not seek contact. It seeks distance.

But the most striking pattern?

Witnesses describe not seeing just one type of creature—but several.

Temagami isn't home to one mystery.

It's home to many.

6. The Bigfoot Connection

Although this book covers a wide range of unexplained phenomena—shadow figures, strange lights, lake creatures, reality anomalies—the core sightings still point toward something resembling the classic description of Bigfoot.

Huge.Upright.Muscular.Silent.Dark.Apex-level awareness.

But Temagami's version is not the gentle giant portrayed in films or the comedic mascot of Pacific Northwest culture.

The Temagami variety is:

- more cautious

- more territorial

- more elusive

- more intimidating

- and often accompanied by **secondary phenomena** like mimicry, wood knocks, low growls, and pacing behavior.

Many witnesses describe feeling a presence long before they hear it.Some feel watched hours before the figure appears.

Others never see anything at all—only hear footsteps large enough to snap trees the thickness of a wrist.

7. When Multiple Mysteries Overlap

What makes Temagami unique is not just the number of sightings —it's the *diversity* of them.

Consider this:

- Bigfoot-like creatures are reported throughout the forest.

- Large wolf-like animals—too big to be wolves—appear at night along certain ridges.

- Strange lights hover over black lakes.

- Voices call from places no human stands.

- Drums echo through fog at dawn.

- Trails vanish or shift beneath the feet of seasoned hikers.

- Entire sections of forest fall silent without explanation.

If this were one phenomenon, it would be easier to categorize.But it isn't.

This is a tapestry of phenomena—each separate, yet oddly connected.

The deeper you go, the more the edges blur.

The shadow figures resemble the giants.The giants seem to follow the drum patterns.The drums appear before time distortions.Time distortions occur near places with heavy mimicry.Mimicry clusters around certain cliffs and valleys where the ridge-walkers appear.

Everything touches everything else.

And that's what makes Temagami unlike any other region in Ontario.Not the sightings themselves—but the **interlocking pattern** behind them.

8. Why Witnesses Stay Silent

One of the strangest parts of investigating Temagami is how many people refuse to talk until they trust you.

A young paddler told me:

"People will think I'm crazy.That's why no one says anything."

A father who watched a massive figure cross a campsite at night said:

"I don't want my kids to think I'm losing it."

A seasoned hunter explained:

"We all know there's something out there.But we don't talk about it because we can't explain it."

And he's right.

Temagami is full of people who have seen things they cannot explain.

And everyone is afraid to be the first to speak.

That silence—decades of it—has allowed the mystery to deepen.

The land has kept its secrets.

And the stories have stayed in the shadows.

Until now.

9. What This Book Will Show You

This book is not about proving anything.It is about revealing a pattern that countless people have lived through—and giving their experiences the respect they deserve.

Over the next 29 chapters, we will examine:

- calls and voices from the forest
- shadow figures watching at night
- giant tracks that vanish mid-stride
- strange lights drifting across blackwater lakes
- lake creatures surfacing beside canoes
- trails that rearrange themselves
- wolves too large to be wolves
- drumming that moves across the fog
- time distortions
- cabin pacing
- mimicry
- near vanishings
- predator behavior with no known predator
- and regions of Temagami that locals warn newcomers to avoid after dark

This isn't cryptid folklore. This is a documented wilderness mystery with enough credible witnesses to fill a courthouse.

Temagami is not like other forests.

It holds something older. Something quieter. Something that watches from behind the pines.

A presence that locals have felt for generations.

And now, through the voices of the people who have encountered it, we will begin to understand the shape of that presence.

10. A Final Thought Before the Descent

If you finish this book with one understanding, let it be this:

Temagami's mystery isn't the creatures. It's the land that shelters them.

This place is ancient. Deep. Silent. Alive in ways that make the modern world feel thin and artificial.

Something walks here. Something hides here. Something listens here.

And whether it's one being or many, one species or a tapestry of them, the truth is the same:

When you step into Temagami, you step into a world that predates us—and isn't all that concerned with being discovered.

CHAPTER 2 — VOICES FROM THE PINES

The Witness Accounts of Impossible Speech Deep in the Temagami Forest

1. When the Forest Knows Your Name

There are a few things people expect to hear in the Temagami backcountry:the wind brushing over Black Spruce, the ticking cadence of a red squirrel, the distant slap of a beaver tail at dusk.

What they *don't* expect—what no one is prepared for—is a human voice calling out from a place where no human should be.

The reports come in from every direction:

Camp leaders.Hunters.Canoeists.Retired rangers.People who know the bush better than most.

And they all say versions of the same unsettling thing:

"Someone called my name from the trees."

Or:

"I heard a person yell 'Hey!' but there was no one there."

Or the quietest, most chilling variation:

"It sounded like someone trying to speak human—but missing something."

These voices aren't distant or echoing.They're close.Personal.Like someone is standing just beyond your headlamp's reach.

Witnesses describe:

- voices with no breath behind them
- words spoken too evenly, without emotion
- short phrases repeated two or three times
- voices that shift position in seconds
- words that sound "practiced," not natural
- tones that mimic someone familiar

No one hears a full sentence.No one hears a conversation.It's always *just enough* to get your attention.

Never enough to feel truly human.

2. The Teenagers at Alex Creek

The first account that convinced me this wasn't simply misheard wind or imagination came from two teenagers—brothers leading a youth canoe trip on Alex Creek, a narrow, winding channel that holds fog like a bowl at dawn.

They were quiet when they told me the story.Not embarrassed.Just troubled.

Around ten at night, after the kids were asleep, the two brothers sat at the fire discussing the next portage. Out of nowhere, a voice called:

"Hey!"

Sharp. Clear. From the treeline behind them.

They assumed a camper had left their tent. But when they checked, everyone was asleep.

Another **"Hey!"** came. This time from the opposite side of camp.

Then a third—closer, quieter, as if spoken directly behind one of the tents.

The younger brother told me:

"It was like a person who didn't understand how to whisper. The tone was wrong. Flat. Like when someone repeats a word they don't know."

They didn't investigate further. They didn't wake the campers. They simply sat up the rest of the night in silence.

The next morning, the forest looked untouched.

But they said the feeling never left. Something in the trees had tested them.

3. Not an Echo — A Response

Even seasoned woodsmen will admit that sound travels strangely across lakes and portages. Echoes can bounce, drift, and warp.

But here's the thing:

Witnesses aren't hearing echoes.

They're hearing **responses**.

This is a pattern that repeats dozens of times across witness accounts:

Someone shouts "Hello?" into the woods — something answers.

A paddler calls to a friend — the same words come back in a different tone.

A portage leader yells "Everyone good?" — and hears a mocking, flat "Good" from behind the trees.

One of the eeriest accounts came from a father camping with his two daughters on a peninsula near Aston Lake. At dusk, the younger girl wandered off to look for firewood. Minutes later, the father heard her voice:

"Dad!"

He called back — but she didn't respond.

He walked thirty meters into the trees and found her crouched by the water, unaware of what he'd heard.

She hadn't called him.

Something else had.

He told me, months later:

"It wasn't just that the voice sounded like her. It was the tone. Too careful. Like something had listened to her talk all day and was trying to get the shape right."

4. The Fog Caller on Angus Lake

Fog and mimicry go together in Temagami like the cold and the pines.

This next account came from a retired OPP officer—someone who had spent years in the north. Practical. No-nonsense. Hard to rattle.

He was finishing a solo trip on Angus Lake when a thick fog rolled in around five a.m. The water went still. The entire world felt suspended.

That's when he heard it:

"Help."

A single word.Monotone.Emotionless.

Not frightened.Not panicked.Not human.

He paddled toward the sound slowly, thinking maybe another soloist was in trouble. But the voice came again—this time from the opposite side of the lake.

"Help."

Same tone.Same wrongness.

He told me:

"A real person begging for help sounds desperate. This sounded like someone who'd never heard desperation trying to imitate it."

He turned back.Left camp early.Didn't look over his shoulder.

When someone with decades of northern experience tells you something shook them—that's enough.

5. The Cabin Voice That Spoke Twice

One of the clearest, most detailed reports came from an older couple who own a cabin accessible only by boat. They've been visiting the same shoreline for thirty years without incident.

Then one September night, just after the fire died, they heard a man's voice outside the cabin:

"Hey."

The husband stood, thinking a late-season paddler had gotten lost.

"Hey," the voice repeated, quieter this time.

He opened the cabin door and shone his flashlight into the darkness.Nothing.

But both of them swore the voice had been less than twenty feet away.

The next morning, their cabin steps had impressions in the moss— two large ovals, spaced far apart, as if something heavy had stood there long enough to flatten the ground but leave no clear print.

The wife said:

"I've heard plenty of men say 'hey' in my life. This wasn't one of them. It sounded like the word without the person."

6. A Voice With No Emotion Is Not Human

Here's something almost every witness says, even if they struggle to articulate it:

The voice has no emotion.

Human voices carry:

- anger
- fear
- confusion
- warmth
- fatigue
- impatience
- personality

Even when someone speaks in a monotone, there's still breath behind it—life, depth, air.

But the voices people hear in Temagami?

They're flat.Hollow.Untextured.

As if something is practicing the sound of a word, not speaking it.

A young guide from Hamilton described it perfectly:

"It sounded like the idea of a voice, not an actual voice."

When so many unrelated people describe the exact same unnatural quality, it's time to consider the possibility that something is deliberately imitating us.

Not perfectly.Not maliciously.

Just… wrong.

7. Bigfoot and the Voice Phenomenon

While this book covers many unexplained events—lights, shadows, massive wolves—there's no denying that some aspects of these voice encounters overlap strongly with Bigfoot behavior.

Across North America, the "Sasquatch mimicry" pattern has been documented for decades:

- imitating human voices
- repeating one or two words
- copying the sound of a person calling
- using mimicry to test or lure
- approaching camps after vocalizations
- reproducing the sound of children
- pacing out of sight while calling

Many witnesses in Temagami describe hearing the voice immediately before:

- footsteps
- tree breaks
- low grunts
- rocks hitting water
- wood-knocking
- something large pacing the perimeter of camp

Some describe the order like this:

1. Voice.

2. Silence.

3. Footsteps.

Others report the opposite:

1. Footsteps.

2. Voice.

Either way, the pairing is too consistent to dismiss.

It is entirely possible that the beings responsible for Temagami's sightings are testing the boundaries of human recognition—learning how we call to each other, how we react to certain words, how we search when a familiar voice calls out.

This isn't folklore. This is a repeating, documented behavior.

8. When the Forest Repeats You

One of the strangest patterns involves what I call **"reflected speech."**

This is when the forest repeats something the witness just said—with perfect timing, but the wrong tone.

A group of paddlers approaching a portage called out:

"Almost there!"

From behind them, deep in the bush:

"Almost there."

Same phrase.Wrong inflection.No breath.

A teacher leading a canoe trip said:

"Everybody stay close."

From the treeline:

"Stay close."

A shaky, emotionless version of his voice.

When I interviewed him, he couldn't explain it. He was a no-nonsense guy—one of those people who laughs at ghost stories.

But this?

This rattled him.

"Whatever it was didn't understand the meaning. It was copying the shape of the words, not the intent."

This is one of the reasons I believe these encounters aren't just auditory hallucinations or echoing illusion.Something is paying attention.Something is listening.And something is trying—however poorly—to speak in a human way.

9. The Line Between Voice and Lure

Most witnesses say the voices are unsettling.Some say they're creepy.A few say they felt nothing at all—just confusion.

But there is one category of witness who feels something different:

Fear.

Not because the voice was loud.Not because it was aggressive.

Because it was *too close*.

One hunter told me:

"It whispered my name. My name. And I don't know how it knew it."

Another:

"The voice wanted me to step into the trees."

A third:

"It was testing me. Seeing how far I'd go."

Some of these encounters feel like a lure.

Not a trap, necessarily.But something probing human behavior.

What will you do when a voice calls out?Will you follow?Will you respond?Will you investigate?

If the beings behind these voices are intelligent—and the patterns strongly suggest they are—then mimicry might serve a purpose:

It may be their way of tracking, studying, or controlling human movement.

Whatever the case, the forest knows how to get your attention.

10. The Unsettling Truth About Voices in Temagami

By now, after hearing dozens of witness accounts and reviewing historical patterns, one conclusion is impossible to ignore:

The voices are real.

They are not hallucinations.

They are not echoes.

They are not misheard animals.

They are a phenomenon with:

- consistency
- repetition
- intention
- geographical clustering
- predictable behavior patterns

And they align with known Bigfoot-like activity documented across North America.

But Temagami's version feels older.Colder.Less human.

Almost as if something has lived here long enough to study the human voice—but not long enough to master it.

This chapter sets the foundation for the auditory mystery. The next dives into the **visual one**—the figures that watchers describe standing in the shadows, on ridges, or between the ancient pines.

CHAPTER 3 — THE WATCHERS OF THE DEEP WOODS
Witness Reports of Tall, Motionless Figures Observing Camps, Trails, and Lakeshores

1. The Feeling of Eyes on You

There are moments in the Temagami backcountry when everything becomes still.No wind.No birds.No insects.No movement in the canopy or the undergrowth.

A silence that feels less like the absence of sound and more like the presence of something watching.

Every paddler I've spoken with—every hunter, every ranger, every solo tripper—knows this silence. They describe it with the same strained voice, as if remembering the exact moment the sensation hit.

You feel a pressure between the shoulder blades.A tightening in the gut.A prickling on the back of the neck.

Not fear—**awareness.**

The instinctive knowledge that someone is standing just outside your field of vision.

This sensation is the first sign of what dozens of witnesses later describe:

Tall figures.Dark forms.Motionless silhouettes standing among the pines.

The Watchers.

2. The Shadow on the Hill Above Whitefish Bay

The clearest account of a Watcher came from a group of high-school canoeists traveling through Whitefish Bay on a late-August evening. The sky was a pale gold, the lake calm as glass.

The group beached their canoes and began setting up camp. One of the leaders walked inland to find a better spot for the food barrel. When he returned, he was pale.

"There's a guy watching us from the hill," he said.

The other leader followed him back up the ridge.

At the top, maybe forty meters away, stood a tall figure. Perfectly still.Broad-shouldered.Dark against the fading sky.Motionless.

Too tall to be a man.Too wide in the torso.Arms hanging low.

As the two leaders watched, the figure didn't move. Didn't flinch. Didn't shift weight. It simply stood there, outlined by the dying light.

When they finally turned away to retreat down the hill, the figure remained frozen.

When they looked back moments later—it was gone.

No footsteps.No sound.No movement through the brush.

Just empty space.

The older of the two leaders told me:

"It wasn't a bear. And it wasn't a person. Whatever it was, it didn't care we were there. It was just… observing."

3. Hunters Who Know the Woods Don't Make Mistakes

Hunters are among the most credible witnesses when it comes to shadow figures. They know animal silhouettes the way a mechanic knows the shape of an engine. They don't mistake a moose for a bear, or a bear for a human.

And yet several experienced Temagami hunters have told me nearly identical stories.

One man, approaching a ridge near Sharp Rock Inlet at sunset, saw a silhouette standing on the crest. It was enormous—tall as a doorway, but narrow in the waist, with long arms that hung much lower than a person's.

He raised his binoculars.

Nothing.

Just darkness in the shape of something upright.

He lowered the binoculars.Looked again with the naked eye.Gone.

No crashing brush.No retreating footsteps.No sound of movement.

Just the ridge, empty and silent.

His voice shook when he told me:

"People don't move like that. Animals don't stand like that. It wasn't supposed to be there."

Another hunter described a similar figure observing him from between two birches. He said it blended with the shadows perfectly until it shifted slightly—just enough for him to recognize that something solid was standing there.

When he blinked, it was gone. He never heard it leave.

Hunters rarely scare easily.

But every one of these men described the same emotion:

They felt judged. Like they had trespassed onto someone else's ground.

4. The Silhouettes That Appear at Dusk

Most Watcher sightings occur during a very specific window:

30 minutes before sunset. 30 minutes after sunset.

This is the period when the forest is neither fully lit nor fully dark—when shadows stretch, contrast softens, and the human eye struggles to separate shape from imagination.

Here's the thing: these sightings are *not* imagination.

Witnesses describe:

- figures too tall to be human
- figures standing absolutely still
- silhouettes that appear on ridges, points, and between pines

- shapes seen across calm lakes at dusk
- figures that vanish without a sound

Some describe the figures as:

solid — blocking light
dense — darker than the forest around them
matte — absorbing light instead of reflecting it
silent — never shifting weight, never snapping a twig
aware — angled slightly toward the witness, never away

A canoeist who saw one across a narrow lake said:

"It looked like someone covered in dark cloth. No details. Just a shape. A wrong shape."

He said the figure remained still the entire time he watched it—until he blinked. Then it was gone.

He paddled out immediately, refusing to sleep on that lake.

5. The Ridge Walker of Anima Nipissing

One of the oldest-known Watcher reports comes from the Anima Nipissing area, where generations of paddlers have described "the Ridge Walker."

The Ridge Walker appears:

- on cliff edges
- above campsites
- along narrow ridgelines
- at great distance

- always upright
- always silhouetted
- always watching

A father and son saw it while cooking dinner at a lakeside firepit. The son pointed out a tall figure standing against the sky on a ridge maybe 300 meters away.

The father assumed it was a hiker. Until it didn't move. At all.

For nearly a full minute.

No shifting. No stepping. No sway. No sign of breath.

Nothing human stands that still.

Then the figure dropped—not backward, not forward—but straight down behind the ridge.

As if it had simply folded into the earth.

The father told me:

"It wasn't just watching. It was waiting."

For what? They didn't stay to find out.

6. The Silent Ones of Temagami

Several witnesses use this phrase without knowing others have used it:

"The Silent One."

They're describing the same phenomenon:

A figure that moves without sound.

One man from North Bay was sitting beside a fallen log near a portage when he saw something move behind a birch tree. He assumed it was a moose. But when the shape stepped out, it wasn't an animal.

It was tall.Lean.Upright.Dark.

It took three steps—fast but smooth.Then disappeared behind a pine.

He stood, expecting to hear it plow through underbrush.

Nothing.Not one twig snapped.

He said:

"It moved like a shadow pretending to be solid."

That phrase stuck with me.

Not a shadow.Not a person.But something trying to inhabit both worlds.

7. The Watchers and the Campfire Rule

One of the patterns that emerges when you read dozens of reports is something I call **the campfire rule.**

Here's how it works:

You don't see the Watchers while the fire is strong.You see them when the fire becomes coals.

The moment the flame dies into a soft orange glow, the forest reveals its shapes.

Nearly every sighting occurs when:

- the fire is low
- the light is weak
- darkness is just settling
- the witness is tired, but still alert
- the world is quiet enough to feel strange

A group of paddlers near Diamond Lake had a moment that illustrates this perfectly. They were sharing a late-night tea when one of them noticed a silhouette standing between two white pines on the opposite shore.

It wasn't there earlier.It wasn't moving.It was simply there.

They whispered to each other, trying to decide whether to shine a light on it.

Before they could agree, the figure turned.

Not stepped.Not shifted.

Turned.

A single movement, so slow and smooth it felt deliberate.

Then it melted into the dark, like ink being absorbed by paper.

None of them slept that night.

One of them told me later:

"It was waiting for the fire to die down. Like it needed a certain darkness."

8. Are These Figures Bigfoot? Or Something Else?

Temagami's Watchers share similarities with traditional Bigfoot sightings:

- tall
- upright
- massive
- broad-chested
- quiet
- observed from a distance

But there are differences, too.

Many witnesses describe the Watchers as:

- thinner than a typical Bigfoot
- less muscular
- more shadow-like
- unnaturally silent
- appearing at greater distance

- moving in impossible ways

The Watchers also show:

- no visible facial detail
- no glowing eyes
- no audible breath
- no reaction to human presence

They don't flee. They don't roar. They don't pace.

They simply *watch*.

Some researchers believe these beings are the same species reported across the continent, just behaving differently in this region.

Others think the Watchers are something else entirely—something overlapping Bigfoot territory, but not Bigfoot themselves.

A long-time trapper from the Lady Evelyn region put it bluntly:

"Whatever those things are, they aren't the big ones. The big ones move. These don't. They're something different."

9. The Watching Is the Message

The most haunting part of these encounters isn't the figure itself. It's what witnesses feel in the moments they lock eyes—or try to.

Because the Watchers don't just stand there. They **observe.**

People describe the sensation like this:

- "It felt like it was reading me."
- "It was waiting to see what I'd do."
- "It didn't move, but I knew it wasn't confused. It knew exactly what I was."
- "It felt like being judged."
- "I was trespassing. That's the only way to phrase it."

These are not jump-scare creatures.They're not predators stalking prey.

They're sentinels.Boundary keepers.

Something ancient.Something old enough to recognize humans—not as threats, but as visitors.

Visitors who sometimes wander too close to whatever they guard.

10. Why These Sightings Matter

As unsettling as these encounters are, they're crucial to understanding the broader Temagami mystery.

Because the Watchers represent the **visual counterpart** to the voices from Chapter 2.

The voices engage.The Watchers observe.

One interacts.The other studies.

Together, they form a pattern far too deliberate to ignore.

This chapter lays the foundation for what comes next:

- the footprints
- the pacing
- the knocks
- the drumming
- the trails that vanish

Each phenomenon reinforces the others.

And all of them point toward the same conclusion:

Temagami is not just home to the unexplained—it is shaped by it.

And whatever moves through those deep forest shadows…knows more about us than we know about them.

CHAPTER 4 — THE BIGFOOT PATTERN BEGINS

How Decades of Tracks, Sightings, and Behavior Form a Single, Coherent Mystery in Temagami

1. When the Stories Stop Being Just Stories

When people talk about Bigfoot in Ontario, the conversation usually drifts toward pop culture—grainy videos online, campfire jokes, or distant rumors. But in Temagami, the tone is different.

Here, the stories aren't jokes.They're told quietly.Privately.Sometimes reluctantly.

And they all carry the same weight: certainty.

Not "I think I saw something."Not "Maybe it was a bear."

But:

"I know what I saw."

Temagami is not a region where people mix up animals.The locals know the difference between:

- a black bear moving upright for a step or two
- a moose seen from the wrong angle
- a person silhouetted on a ridge

These forests are full of people who can identify animals by tracks alone, from twenty feet away, in half light.

So when they describe something that doesn't fit any known animal—something massive, upright, intelligent, and silent—it's worth listening.

This chapter gathers the physical evidence, the track patterns, and the consistency behind eyewitness accounts to show one clear truth:

Whatever is moving through Temagami, it's big, it's smart, and it's been here longer than any of us.

2. When You See the Footprints Before You Hear the Stories

One of the earliest clues I found about Temagami's Bigfoot presence didn't come from a story or a sighting.

It came from footprints.

Long before people reported tall silhouettes or strange calls, they found prints along muddy portages and secluded lakeshores. Some described them timidly, afraid of sounding foolish. Others laughed nervously when they told me, as if trying to convince themselves the prints weren't real.

But the details were consistent:

- 14 to 18 inches long
- wide, deep impressions
- clear mid-foot flexibility

- no claw marks

- enormous stride length (sometimes over six feet)

- clear push-off toes

And most importantly:

The prints didn't behave like bear tracks.

A retired guide showed me a sketch from the 1990s—two prints found near the portage into Kokoko Bay. The stride was too long for any human, the weight too heavy for a hiker, and the prints far too human-like to belong to a bear.

He told me:

"I've guided since the seventies. I know bear tracks. These weren't bears. This was a person-shaped foot the size of a frying pan."

Another set of tracks appeared along a muddy shoreline in mid-April, found by two paddlers who camped early in the season.

The prints were fresh.Deep.Clear.

When they followed them for twenty meters, the tracks simply stopped—mid-stride—at the edge of a granite slab. No return prints, no signs of climbing, no water drag marks.

"Something huge walked across the mud," one of the paddlers said, "and then vanished when it hit the rock."

That's a pattern that repeats itself again and again.

The creature leaves tracks when the ground is soft.When it hits rock, it disappears.

Not because it flew or teleported.Because it knows exactly where to step to leave no trace.

That's not an animal's behavior.

That's an intelligent being's behavior.

3. The Sighting That Opens the Door

There are always two types of Bigfoot sightings:

1. sightings where people catch a glimpse

2. sightings where people lock eyes with something that shouldn't exist

The second type changes people.

One of the most compelling examples came from a Temagami Fire Ranger who encountered a massive figure near a lookout point off a narrow access road.

He said:

"It was maybe eighty yards away. Standing. Not hunched. Upright.

I thought it was a person at first—maybe a hiker in a dark jacket. But the proportions were wrong. The torso was too thick. The arms hung too low.

Then it stepped away from the tree. And the whole tree shook."

He told me he didn't feel fear.He felt something closer to awe.

A presence so physically overwhelming that it didn't need to threaten him.

It simply existed.

When he looked down to step around a rock and glanced back up, the creature was gone.

But the tree it had leaned on still swayed.

4. The Behavior That Matches No Known Animal

Temagami's Bigfoot behavior is shockingly consistent with reports from the Pacific Northwest, Alaska, and even northern Minnesota.

Witnesses describe the same patterns:

A. Avoidance, Not Aggression

The creatures don't charge, stalk, or attack. They observe. Circle camps. Watch from ridges. Move away when noticed.

B. Stealth That Shouldn't Be Possible

People hear them only when they want you to hear them.

One witness said:

"It broke a sapling, walked five steps loud enough to shake the ground—then nothing. Total silence. Like it dissolved."

C. Intelligence in Movement

They use:

- ridgelines

- old-growth valleys
- fog
- wind direction
- waterways

to move unseen.

No animal on the continent moves with that level of strategy.

D. Curiosity About Humans

Not playful.Not taunting.

But curious.

About our camps.Our food barrels.Our conversations.Our routines.

People report sensing they're being observed long before a sighting happens.

E. They Don't Run From Humans. They Step Away.

Witnesses don't see a blur or a panicked bolt.They see one or two long, smooth steps—and the creature is gone.

Like a ghost with muscle mass.

5. The Long History Temagami Never Advertised

Bigfoot sightings in this region didn't begin with modern YouTubers or social media.

They go back more than a century.

In the 1920s: Prospectors reported "large, barefoot men" at the edges of their work camps.

In the 1940s: Loggers spoke of "tall, silent figures" watching from treelines.

In the 1960s: A group of canoeists described seeing a "black giant" cross a portage trail at dawn.

In the 1980s: Several cabins in the North Arm area reported food barrels moved or overturned—with large prints found nearby.

In the early 2000s: Hikers near Spawning Lake heard wood-knocks followed by heavy steps pacing the ridge.

And in the last decade? Sightings have increased.

Not because the creatures became more active—but because the number of people traveling deep into Temagami with smartphones, GPS units, and GoPros has increased.

Technology hasn't caught these beings.

It has simply revealed how often they are near us.

6. The Woman on the Pink Granite Shoreline

This is the sighting that convinced me Temagami's Bigfoot mystery is more than scattered stories.

A woman and her husband were paddling across a wide, calm bay. The sun was low, painting the granite pink.

As they drifted, she noticed movement on the opposite shoreline—something stepping from behind a large cedar.

She assumed it was a moose. Until it stood upright.

Tall. Broad. Covered in dark, coarse hair. Long arms. A head that seemed lower on the shoulders than a human's.

She said:

"It walked out like it had every right to be there. Not scared. Not hiding."

It took three steps to cross an open outcrop—steps longer than her entire canoe.

Then it turned and slipped behind the treeline.

The whole encounter lasted maybe five seconds. But she remembered every second of it.

Her voice cracked when she said:

"It wasn't a person. I know what I saw. And I think it saw us first."

Her husband, a quiet man, said nothing during the interview. But when I asked him if he believed what his wife saw, he simply nodded and looked at the floor.

People who lie don't react that way. People who are telling the truth often do.

7. Why the Sightings Are So Consistent

After years of collecting stories, one question remained:

Are these people seeing the same creature or the same species?

Here's what the data suggests:

HEIGHT:

7 to 9 feet tall.

BUILD:

Massive, barrel-chested, long arms.

HEAD SHAPE:

Slightly conical or rounded, set low in the shoulders.

MOVEMENT:

Smooth, quick, shockingly silent.

HAIR:

Dark brown, black, or deep rust.

EYES:

Dark, reflective, not glowing.

BEHAVIOR:

Avoidant, observant, strategic.

FOOTPRINTS:

Human-like, but much larger, with mid-foot flexibility.

These traits match reports from across North America, which adds weight to the idea that a single, widespread species exists—and prefers deep forested regions with limited human development.

Temagami, with its endless old growth and complex geography, is the perfect habitat.

8. When the Tracks Lead Nowhere

Another repeated pattern involves tracks that start and stop abruptly.

Several groups have reported finding massive prints:

- in deep moss
- in soft mud
- on sandy shores

…but then the prints end at a:

- granite slab
- fallen log
- ridge edge
- creek bed
- cluster of roots

A moose leaves a mess when it climbs rocks. A bear leaves claws, drag marks, and weight shifts.

These creatures leave nothing.

It's as if they understand precisely where to step to erase evidence.

One tracker from Sudbury described following a trail of enormous prints for nearly a hundred meters before they ended abruptly at the base of a ridge.

He said:

"It walked straight up the rock. Didn't stumble. Didn't slip. Didn't leave so much as a scuff mark. Whatever it was moved like it knew exactly where to place its feet."

This is the kind of behavior you'd expect from:

- a human with extreme training
- a predator with unmatched stealth
- or an intelligent being accustomed to hiding in plain sight

Not from any known animal in Canada.

9. The Witnesses Aren't Seeing One Creature — They're Seeing a Pattern

This chapter isn't about one sighting or one set of prints.It's about the **consistency** behind all of them.

Dozens of unrelated people described:

- tall upright beings

- quiet movement
- disappearing tracks
- massive silhouettes
- heavy pacing outside camps
- mimicry paired with sightings
- wood-knocks followed by visual encounters

The species—whatever it is—appears to:

- travel along ridges
- use shorelines at dusk
- approach camps out of curiosity
- watch humans from distance
- stay hidden unless cornered
- communicate through knocks, whistles, or mimicry

And most importantly:

It avoids confrontation at all costs.

That's not the behavior of a monster. It's the behavior of an intelligent creature that wants to remain unseen.

10. What This Chapter Points Toward

When you assemble all the stories, tracks, and sightings, one conclusion becomes impossible to avoid:

Temagami hosts a population of large, intelligent, elusive forest beings—commonly called Bigfoot—that behave with intention, caution, and awareness of humans.

This isn't myth. This isn't folklore. This isn't exaggeration.

It's a pattern.

A documented, consistent, multi-decade pattern across hundreds of witnesses.

And it forms the backbone of the Temagami mystery.

In the next chapter, we move deeper into that mystery—into the sounds, signals, and behaviors used by these beings to communicate.

Wood knocks. Rhythmic signals. Pacing. Drumming.

The physical signs come first. The auditory clues come next.

And that is where the forest begins to speak.

CHAPTER 5 — THE DRUMS, THE WHISTLES, THE SIGNALS

How Sound Becomes the First Warning — or Invitation — in the Temagami Backcountry

1. Sounds That Don't Belong to the North Woods

Most people expect noise in the Temagami wilderness.

Waves slapping rock. Loons echoing across the lake at dusk. A distant chainsaw drifting from someone's cabin. Canoes bumping gently in the water.

What no one expects–what no paddler, guide, or hunter is prepared for–is a sudden, perfectly timed **knock**, or a deep **thoom** echoing across still water, or a **whistle** that seems to follow the group along a shoreline.

These signals come in patterns:

- **single knocks**
- **double knocks**
- **slow drum beats**
- **sharp whistles**
- **three-note sequences**
- **knocking that responds to you**

- **water slaps too heavy for beavers**

And they arrive with eerie consistency **before** or **after** sightings of tall figures or other unexplained events.

Witnesses say the same thing, in slightly different ways:

"The forest was talking to itself."

Or:

"It was signaling something. I just don't know what."

These sounds are not random. They are not natural. And they occur far too frequently to be coincidence.

2. The First Wood-Knock: A Paddler's Turning Point

The first time I spoke with someone who heard a true Temagami wood-knock—one of the classic signals associated with Bigfoot encounters across North America—it wasn't a sensational moment. It was strangely matter-of-fact.

The witness was a soft-spoken teacher from North Bay who took his students on wilderness trips every summer.

His story began like this:

"It was around 8 p.m. We'd just finished cleaning up. I tossed a piece of deadfall into the bush, and a second later—**KNOCK.** One solid hit. And it wasn't an echo."

He clapped his hands sharply when he told me the story, imitating the sound.

"It didn't ring like hitting a tree with a stick. It thudded, like someone with real force hit the side of a cedar with a baseball bat."

He tried to dismiss it. The second knock changed everything.

KNOCK. KNOCK. "Two more. Same spot. Same power."

He described a feeling that made him step back instinctively.

"It was answering me. I knew that. Right away."

He didn't see anything. But he didn't need to.

The sound itself had an intelligence behind it. A deliberate timing. A meaning he couldn't understand but couldn't deny.

And he was not alone.

3. The Hunters Who Heard the "Conversation"

Three hunters camping off a remote access road deep in the North Arm area heard what they described as **two unseen beings knocking back and forth across a valley.**

Not random. Not scattered. But organized — rhythmic.

One knock from the left ridge. Two knocks from the right. A pause. Then three faster knocks from the left again.

One of the hunters said:

"It sounded like the hills were speaking to each other."

They tried to explain it away—woodpeckers, falling branches, echoes. But woodpeckers don't knock at night. Branches don't sound intentional. Echoes don't answer each other.

The oldest hunter, a man with fifty years of bush experience, refused to talk about it after that night.

But when he finally told his side, his voice dropped to almost a whisper:

"Whatever it was… they were coordinating."

This is one of the patterns that emerges repeatedly in Temagami:

the sound isn't random—it's relational.

Something is communicating.

4. The Whistle That Followed the Portage Group

Whistle encounters are some of the most unnerving because they track people.

A camp leader told me a story that stayed with me for months afterward. His group was traveling a long portage near Kokoko Lake. The trail was narrow and quiet, with dense undergrowth on both sides.

Halfway through the trail, someone whistled:

Two notes. Soft. Clean.

He assumed it was one of the campers. But none of the kids reacted — no one looked over their shoulder, no one smiled, no one answered.

They kept walking.

Another whistle. Farther up the trail. Then another from behind.

It followed them the entire rest of the portage — never close enough to see, but close enough to feel monitored.

One of the campers whispered:

"It's pacing us."

The leader admitted to me:

"I've heard all kinds of birds whistle. This wasn't a bird. It was too… accurate."

Nearly every whistle encounter has the same eerie detail:

It sounds almost human, but not quite. Too pure. Too controlled. Too perfectly spaced.

Like something imitating a whistle mechanically. Deliberately.

5. The Drum That Moved Across the Lake

Of all the auditory encounters, the drum is perhaps the most unsettling.

Not a cultural drum. Not a hand-drum. Not thunder.

A single, deep, resonant **THOOM** that travels across lakes at dawn or dusk.

One couple staying on a remote island on Obabika Lake heard it at six in the morning—a low fog hugging the water.

THOOM.

A second one, farther left.

THOOM.

Then one behind them.

The husband described it:

"It wasn't echoing. It was moving."

The wife said:

"It felt like the water itself was vibrating."

When they paddled out that morning, the lake was silent, perfectly calm. No cabins nearby. No camps. No boats.

They never heard it again.

Drums usually occur in clusters of two or three. Never one long sequence. Never chaotic.

Always slow. Always calculated. Always heavy.

They seem to serve a purpose—though what that purpose is, no one has figured out.

6. Signals Before Sightings: The Pattern No One Talks About

One of the clearest patterns in Temagami is this:

Knocks, whistles, or drums often occur right before someone sees a figure.

A man hears three knocks on a distant ridge — and twenty minutes later a tall silhouette crosses a portage trail.

A group hears a whistle near sunset — and a dark figure appears on a cliff above their campsite.

A drum echoes across a bay — and a massive shape steps between two pines on the opposite shore.

Witnesses don't know these stories ahead of time. They're not primed, misled, or spooked by rumors.

But their experiences line up in a way that suggests the sounds serve a role.

Possibilities include:

- **communication between beings**
- **territorial warnings**
- **signals for movement**
- **testing human reactions**
- **locational markers**

The exact meaning remains unknown.

But the pattern is unmistakable.

7. The Pacer: When Footsteps Replace Words

There is one auditory phenomenon that sits at the boundary between sound and presence:**the Pacer.**

Nearly every region in Temagami has at least one account of something **walking circles around a campsite**—but never entering.

Heavy, bipedal steps:

- slow
- steady
- deliberate
- pacing the perimeter

One group near Diamond Lake heard footsteps circling their camp for nearly forty minutes.

Not a bear.Not a moose.

A creature walking on two feet.Never brushing against tents.Never snapping twigs the way a large animal would.

Just smooth, heavy, rhythmic pacing.

The leader told me:

"Bears meander. This was a walk. A real walk. Like someone patrolling."

Pacing often follows knocks or whistles.

The signals come first. Then the presence.

It's as if the forest is announcing something—and then that something arrives.

8. Why These Sounds Don't Fit Normal Wildlife

Skeptics often ask why these sounds can't be attributed to:

- owls
- ravens
- loons
- wolves
- woodpeckers
- beavers
- falling branches
- echo effects

But here's why the explanations don't work:

1. Woodpeckers don't knock once.

And they don't hit trees at night.

2. Beavers slap water, not wood.

And their slaps are unmistakably wet.

3. Birds whistle—but not like this.

Temagami whistles are too clean, too deliberate, too controlled.

4. Trees falling don't create repeating patterns.

5. Echoes don't answer back.

6. Animals don't communicate across ridges with rhythmic knocking.

7. No known species coordinates movement with sound signals.

Unless…

Unless what people are hearing isn't wildlife.Unless it's something else entirely.

9. The Intelligence Behind the Noise

After interviewing dozens of witnesses and mapping out clusters of auditory reports, the conclusion is difficult to avoid:

These signals are intentional.Thought-out.Coordinated.And tied to an intelligent presence.

This intelligence shows itself through:

- **timing** — knocks that answer human noises
- **pattern** — whistles spaced evenly
- **coordination** — drums responding from different sides
- **selective silence** — stopping the moment a human investigates
- **testing** — repeating a sound after a human repeats it

Something is using sound the way humans use radios, hand signals, or whistles.

Not randomly. But with purpose.

10. What the Signals Reveal About the Temagami Mystery

This chapter doesn't solve anything.

But it adds a crucial layer to the larger pattern unfolding in this book.

Because when you put all the auditory events together:

- knocks
- whistles
- drums
- pacing

- water slaps
- breathy grunts
- unnatural silence

…you begin to see the outline of a system.

A communication network.

A set of rules.

A presence that talks, warns, tests, and coordinates.

What watches Temagami at night is not just physical.It is **aware**.

And the signals are its first language.

In the next chapter, we step into how the forest's path—and time itself—sometimes bends in impossible ways.

A place where trails shift.Distances warp.And people walk forward only to find themselves behind where they started.

CHAPTER 6 — TRAILS THAT AREN'T THERE TOMORROW

Witness Accounts of Paths That Shift, Loops That Shouldn't Exist, and Forests That Move When You Aren't Looking

1. When a Familiar Trail Stops Being Familiar

Every Temagami paddler knows the feeling of stepping onto a portage they've walked a dozen times before. You know every bend, every patch of mud, every log you've tripped over year after year.

So when one of those trails suddenly looks unfamiliar—when the trees feel different, when the ground slopes the wrong way, when the markers aren't where they should be—you know something is wrong.

Ask around quietly and you'll find a surprising number of people who've had the same experience:

The trail shifts. Not dramatically. Not with fanfare. Just… enough.

Enough to make a seasoned woodsman stop mid-step and say:

"This wasn't like this yesterday."

Or:

"Where the hell is the trail?"

And in the darkest accounts:

"I walked twenty minutes before I realized the forest had changed around me."

These aren't rookies. They aren't tourists. They're guides, hunters, rangers, and lifelong paddlers.

People who *don't* get lost.

And yet Temagami manages to disorient them in ways no one can fully explain.

2. The Portage That Turned Into Forest

One of the most credible accounts came from a pair of brothers who'd been canoeing the region since childhood. They were carrying gear along a short 400-meter portage they'd walked dozens of times.

Halfway through, the trail simply… ended.

Not faded. Ended.

One moment they were on a clear dirt path. The next, they were standing in unbroken undergrowth.

They looked behind them—the trail was still there. They looked ahead—nothing.

No markers. No worn path. No disturbed moss.

Just a wall of cedar and spruce.

They stood there confused for a long minute before turning around. But when they walked back toward the lake, something was wrong again.

The trail behind them was now slightly altered:

- rocks they didn't recognize
- roots that seemed out of place
- a bend where there hadn't been one

One of the brothers said:

"It felt like we'd walked into a version of the forest that wasn't ours."

When they finally reached the lake, they were shaken. They never used that portage again.

3. When Time Slips While the Trail Moves

Many of the trail-shifting accounts have another unsettling piece: time doesn't add up.

A group of four university students hiked a portage that should take twenty minutes. They emerged ninety minutes later—even though none of them remembered stopping.

No one argued. No one daydreamed. No one wandered off.

It was as if the trail absorbed an hour of their lives.

When they checked their watches at the next lake, they didn't believe the time. One said:

"We didn't walk that long. I'd bet my tuition money on it."

Time loss in Temagami doesn't feel supernatural when you read about it academically.But when four level-headed adults look genuinely shaken because their internal clocks don't match the watches on their wrists—that's different.

It's not fear of being lost.It's fear of reality not aligning with memory.

4. Trails That Loop Back to the Beginning

On the east side of Lake Temagami, there's a particular portage that locals warn first-time travelers about—not because it's hard, but because it plays tricks.

A man from Sudbury told me he walked this portage with his young son. At some point, the trail branched. He didn't remember the fork from previous years, but he trusted the right-hand route.

After twenty minutes, they stepped out onto a lakeshore.

Not the lake they were heading toward—the lake they had just come from.

He and his son stared at the canoes resting on the sand.

He said:

"I felt stupid. Like we'd made some obvious mistake.

But here's the thing—my son said he never saw a fork."

That detail matters.

One of them saw a fork.One didn't.

Both ended up back where they started.

This is one of the eeriest consistencies in these reports:

Two people walking the same path sometimes experience it differently. One sees splits, structures, or landmarks. The other insists they weren't there.

It's as if the forest shows a slightly different version of itself to each person.

Not illusion. Not hallucination.

A shifting reality.

5. The Ranger Who Stopped Walking Mid-Step

One of the most experienced people I spoke with—a retired fire ranger—encountered something he still can't explain after forty years on the land.

He was walking a short portage near Sharp Rock Inlet when he stepped over a root he'd stepped over countless times before.

Except… the root wasn't there.

He froze mid-step, suddenly off balance. The root he was expecting simply didn't exist.

He looked down—only moss.

He looked up—the next fifty meters of trail looked subtly wrong. The slope. The spacing of the trees. The absence of a familiar boulder.

He said:

"It was the same trail, but it wasn't."

He backed away slowly, refusing to turn his back.

When he reached the last familiar landmark, he looked forward again—

—and the trail was normal.

He told me:

"I never believed in anything strange until that moment. That was the day the land blinked."

6. When the Forest "Closes" Around People

Several witnesses describe the forest becoming claustrophobic—like the trees tighten around the trail.

Not like a panic attack. Not atmospheric pressure.

Physical space changes:

- trees appear closer
- branches seem to narrow
- the path feels squeezed
- sightlines shorten unnaturally

A camp leader described a section of trail so tight he felt he had to turn sideways—even though he'd walked that trail before and knew it wasn't narrow.

A group of paddlers described a section of old-growth forest that "felt like a hallway," as if the trunks were forming walls.

One woman put it bluntly:

"The forest didn't want us there. That's the only way I can explain it."

This phenomena often comes with other signs:

- sudden silence
- a feeling of being observed
- subtle disorientation
- trails that feel longer or shorter than they should

And most unnervingly:

the sensation disappears the moment you turn around.

Walk back ten steps, and the "tightness" evaporates.

Turn forward again—and it returns.

Almost like a presence pressing inward.

7. The Disappearing Marker Phenomenon

Portage markers in Temagami range from faded paint on trees to old tin can lids nailed into bark decades ago. They're subtle, but experienced paddlers know how to spot them.

And yet, dozens of witnesses say the same thing:

The markers were there—until they weren't.

Not removed. Not fallen. Not aged away.

Just... gone.

A group of four paddlers saw a clear marker on a cedar at the beginning of a trail. Halfway through, they reached a junction and turned left, expecting another marker. Nothing.

They walked thirty meters back to the previous junction—and the first marker was gone too.

All four insisted they'd seen it. All four were experienced.

A review of the trail later that summer found all markers intact and exactly where they had always been.

So what did the group see?

What didn't they see?

And why did all four people agree on the same false memory?

Unless it wasn't false.

Unless the forest showed them something temporary.

A version of the trail that existed for moments—and then reverted.

8. The Forest That Redirects

One of the strangest and most consistent reports involves trails that *direct* people away from certain areas.

These witnesses all say variations of the same thing:

"The trail didn't want us going that way."

People describe:

- trails subtly shifting down the wrong slope
- clear paths fading only when heading toward certain valleys
- forks appearing only when approaching specific ridges
- forest density increasing in one direction and not the other
- animals behaving abnormally near certain trailheads

Several locations have recurring reports of this behavior.

One camp leader told me:

"Every time we approached that valley, the trail tightened, the forest went silent, and the kids started arguing or tripping on nothing.

The moment we turned back, everything cleared."

Is the land protecting something?Or protecting the humans?

No one knows.

But the pattern is too persistent to dismiss.

9. Are These Trail Distortions Connected to the Beings?

This question came up over and over during interviews:

Are the Bigfoot-like beings causing trail distortions? Or are they simply navigating them?

Three possibilities exist:

Theory 1: The beings know the forest better than we do.

They use ridges, rock shelves, and unseen paths that humans overlook.

Theory 2: The beings influence the land.

This is the more supernatural interpretation—that the presence of these beings distorts perception.

Theory 3: The land itself reacts to presence.

An ancient wilderness with natural anomalies humans haven't mapped or understood.

Most witnesses lean toward a combination of the first and third.

One hunter suggested:

"The forest bends for them, not for us."

Another said:

"It's like they move through a version of the forest we don't have access to."

Whatever the explanation, the result is the same:

Humans walking these trails sometimes slip—not into danger, but into confusion.

A temporary disorientation that feels intentional.

10. When You Step Out and Nothing Matches Your Memory

The scariest stories don't involve being lost.

They involve stepping into somewhere that shouldn't exist.

A young couple near Aston Lake stepped onto a familiar portage and walked for maybe fifteen minutes before realizing the terrain made no sense:

- the old-growth stand was younger
- the ground was softer
- the rock formations were different
- the forest had a faint, unnatural quiet

When they turned around to retrace their steps, the entire trail behind them looked different too.

No landmarks. No familiar bends. Just forest.

They began to panic.

But ten minutes later, the world snapped back. The trail looked normal again.

The woman told me:

"It was like walking into a parallel version of the same forest."

Not supernatural.

Just… wrong.

And then suddenly right again.

11. What This Chapter Tells Us About the Temagami Mystery

This chapter isn't about "getting lost." It's about **the land behaving in ways that don't align with known geography, human perception, or memory.**

Taken alone, each account could be dismissed:

- tired eyes
- fog confusion
- worn-out hikers
- tricky lighting
- similar-looking trees

But taken together?

Across decades?

Across hundreds of witnesses?

A pattern emerges:

**Trails vanish.

Trails reappear.Landmarks change.Distances shift.Time slips.Reality bends, softly and briefly.And people feel watched the entire time.**

And this pattern almost always overlaps with:

- nearby sightings
- mimicry
- knocks
- pacing
- giant tracks
- drumming

The distortions don't replace the physical creatures.

They accompany them.

Temagami is not just home to Bigfoot.

It's home to **a layered, shifting wilderness** where the boundary between the explainable and the inexplicable is thinner than anywhere else in Ontario.

And the deeper you go, the more the forest shows you versions of itself you were never meant to walk through

CHAPTER 7 — TIME MISSING IN THE PINES
Witness Reports of Lost Minutes, Failed Watches, and Moments That Cannot Be Accounted For

1. When Time Slips Out From Under You

There is a particular kind of silence that settles in Temagami's deep woods. Not the natural quiet of early morning, not the muffled calm before rain, but a hard, sudden stillness that feels like it has weight.

This silence has a way of changing time.

People who have spent their entire lives in these forests—guides, trappers, hunters, paddlers—describe moments where the world seems to pause, slow down, or skip forward without warning.

You look at your watch. You carry on. Then suddenly it's an hour later.

No memory. No transition. Just absence.

These aren't dramatic events. There's no light, no dizziness, no blackout.

It's more like stepping over a root and discovering, somehow, that thirty minutes disappeared mid-step.

Not due to exhaustion. Not dehydration. Not cannabis or alcohol.

Clear-headed people—stone sober, well-rested—experience it too often to ignore.

Something in these woods bends time around the edges.Quietly.Gently.But unmistakably.

2. The Missing Forty Minutes on the Red Squirrel Road

A man from Temiskaming Shores was driving along Red Squirrel Road near dusk. He knew the road well—every bend, every washout, every spot where moose liked to cross.

He left the turnoff at exactly 6:20 p.m.He checked because he was timing the drive to a friend's cabin.

The trip should take 25 minutes.It always did.

But when he reached the cabin, the friend was already walking toward the vehicle looking concerned.

"Where the hell were you?" he asked.

The driver looked at his dashboard clock.**7:25 p.m.**

He said:

"An hour? That's not right. That's not possible."

He didn't remember stopping.Didn't remember slowing down.Didn't remember anything unusual at all.

Just driving.Then arriving.

His friend swore he heard a distant engine approaching, then nothing—as if the sound vanished—then the truck reappeared much later.

The driver told me:

"I didn't lose consciousness. I didn't black out. I didn't daydream.

But I can't account for that hour. It simply isn't there."

This pattern repeats again and again in Temagami:

People move normally. Time does not.

3. The Canoeists Who Lost the Sunset

Three university students were paddling through a narrow channel near Wakimika Lake. The sun was low — still above the treeline, still casting gold across the water.

They remember the color. They remember the warmth. They remember the shadows of the pines reaching across the lake.

They turned a corner.

And suddenly the sun was gone.

Not behind a cloud. Not behind a ridge. Gone.

The sky was a darker blue — the kind you see forty minutes after sunset.

The air was cooler. The insects were louder. And their watches all agreed: **8:17 p.m.**

They all remembered checking the time before the bend: **7:30 p.m.**

Forty-seven minutes had passed.

But their paddle strokes hadn't changed. Their conversation hadn't paused. Nothing marked the transition.

One of them said:

"It was like the world skipped forward without us."

Another insisted they'd only paddled for a minute or two since the last time check.

But the light said otherwise. And the clocks matched the light.

This wasn't boredom or distraction. This was a jump.

A missing block of time that no one could feel as it passed.

4. The Guide Who Walked Into a Patch of Stillness

The most reliable witnesses in Temagami are the guides because a guide can't afford to misread the forest.

One experienced canoe guide told me about a moment on a trail near Florence Lake. He walked ahead of his group to scout a tricky incline. The light filtered through the canopy in thin, warm stripes. The air smelled of warm moss and cedar.

He remembers stepping over a fallen log.

Then he remembers standing on the other side of it, feeling… wrong.

Not dizzy. Not injured. Just displaced.

He checked his GPS out of habit.

Twenty-six minutes had passed.

He had no memory of walking anywhere.He hadn't heard his group calling.He hadn't felt time passing.

He said:

"It felt like I walked into a pocket of quiet. And when I walked out of it, the world had moved on without me."

He tried to downplay it, but guides don't imagine lost half-hours.Especially not experienced ones.

5. When Watches Fail Entirely

Electronics dying in the backcountry is normal enough—but not like this.

Not when *only* the watches fail.Not when the failures line up with vanished time.

Dozens of people have described the same phenomenon:

- digital watches freezing
- analog watches stopping
- GPS timestamp errors
- compasses spinning or locking
- phones resetting their internal clocks

These events almost always occur:

- near ridge lines

- in deep valleys
- close to lakes with heavy fog
- after hearing knocking or whistles
- near locations with known sightings

A father and son camping near Aston Lake noticed their watches stopped within the same ten-minute window.

Both.Different brands.Different ages.

One stopped at 2:41 a.m.The other: 2:43 a.m.

When they consulted a third watch in the canoe pack—it too had stopped at 2:42 a.m.

Three watches.Different mechanisms.Same failure window.

The father said:

"It felt like something passed through us. Not physically. But through time."

6. The Missing Hour on Temagami Island

A pair of experienced kayakers exploring Temagami Island stopped at a small sandy patch to stretch and check their gear. They weren't there long. They remember taking off their packs, drinking some water, joking about a trout that stole a lure earlier that day.

They got back in the kayaks, paddled around the point, and continued toward the next campsite.

It was only when they reached the site that they noticed something was wrong.

The sun was much lower.The temperature had dropped.The sky had shifted toward evening.

Their watches said **6:58 p.m.**

They both remembered the last time check vividly: **5:05 p.m.**

They thought maybe their watches were wrong.But both?In sync? By nearly two hours?

They checked their phones.Same time.

The woman told me:

"We weren't tired. We weren't drinking. We weren't confused.

It was like we stepped out of the world for a while."

The man added:

"If something had happened—if we'd slept or fainted or wandered—we would have felt it. But nothing happened. Nothing."

Nothing except two vanished hours.

7. The "Pause" Effect Witnesses Don't Know How to Describe

Some people don't lose time.They feel time… hesitate.

A man from North Bay experienced it while walking a narrow ridge. He described the moment like this:

"I took a step and suddenly everything felt thick. The air. The sound. Even my own movement. Not slow-motion—just heavy."

He said the silence became so deep it felt physical.No breeze.No birds.No insects.

He stood still, unsure why he'd stopped.A moment later, the forest felt normal again.

But when he checked his watch, four minutes had passed.

Four minutes he couldn't feel.

This "pause effect" comes up in many witness interviews:

- birds stop mid-call
- wind dies instantly
- the forest becomes "dense"
- the air feels heavy
- then everything resumes

As if reality flickers.As if the wilderness holds its breath.

8. When Sound Slows Down

Not everyone experiences missing time visually.Some hear it.

Several witnesses have described moments where environmental sound slowed, deepened, or faded unnaturally.

A paddler near the North Arm said:

"The loons sounded wrong. Like they were calling through water."

Another said:

"Our voices felt delayed, like the air was thick."

A hunter described hearing his own breath in strange, stretched-out rhythm, as if the rise and fall of his chest were disconnected from the sound.

He thought it was just his imagination—until his partner said:

"It sounds like the world's under water."

These effects often accompany:

- missing minutes
- sudden silence
- tall figures on ridge lines
- knocks
- whistles
- footprints that appear or vanish

One does not explain the other. But together they form a coherent pattern.

Something that affects sound. Something that affects time.

Something that affects perception.

And all of it happens quietly.

9. Are These Time Events Connected to the Beings?

This is one of the hardest questions to answer.

In some cases, the missing time occurs **with no sighting** and no auditory events.

In others, time loss follows:

- pacing
- knocks
- shadows
- strange lights

And sometimes, the two overlap perfectly:

A group hears a knock…experiences a period of silence…then notices their watches are wrong.

Three theories emerge:

Theory 1 — The beings move in ways that disrupt time perception.

Their presence confuses human senses.

Theory 2 — Humans slip into a natural anomaly in the landscape.

Areas where magnetic fields, geology, and geography create odd pockets.

Theory 3 — The forest itself is layered.

And people occasionally step into a different layer briefly.

None of these are proven.But all three match the evidence better than hallucination or carelessness.

When ten independent witnesses describe the same type of event,you stop doubting the witnessesand start questioning the environment.

10. The Pattern Behind the Missing Minutes

After reviewing dozens of accounts, the pattern becomes difficult to ignore:

Time events occur:

- near old-growth stands
- close to water
- beside cliff lines
- within natural "bowls" of geography
- near known Bigfoot sightings
- after auditory signals
- during heavy fog or stillness

These conditions repeat with unnerving consistency.

People aren't "losing time" because they're confused.

They're losing time because something in the Temagami wilderness affects:

- perception
- awareness
- sound
- orientation
- memory
- internal clocks

Not violently. Not dramatically. Just enough to make reality ripple.

11. What This Chapter Reveals About Temagami

Taken one at a time, these events could be dismissed as fatigue, distraction, or natural error.

But taken together?

Across decades?

Across people who don't know each other?

Across locations that intersect cleanly with other unexplained phenomena?

A picture emerges:

**Temagami is not just a place where creatures hide.

It is a place where time and perception shift around the presence of those creatures.**

Not always.Not predictably.But consistently enough to see the outline of something bigger.

Something the land knows.Something the forest responds to.Something the witnesses feel long before they understand it.

And whatever these beings are — whatever intelligence watches from the ridges and signals through the trees — they're not just physical.

They exist in a space where time bends.

The next chapter takes us deeper into that distorted landscape:

CHAPTER 8 — THE FOREST THAT REARRANGES ITSELF
Witness Encounters With Moving Landmarks, Changing Terrain, and a Wilderness That Doesn't Stay Still

1. When the Land Moves Just Enough to Be Wrong

There's a moment in the deep Temagami backcountry when you realize the forest isn't simply alive with wildlife — it is alive in a different way.Not metaphorically.Not romantically.Literally alive.

People describe it in quiet voices, with a tone that carries more disbelief than fear:

"The trees weren't where they were supposed to be."

"The shoreline shifted."

"That boulder wasn't there yesterday."

"We walked toward the ridge, and the ridge moved."

These aren't exaggerations.They're not hallucinations.And they're not the ramblings of people who were lost or confused.

These are the testimonies of:

- guides
- paddlers

- rangers
- trappers
- firefighters
- experienced backcountry travelers

People who know the land intimately.

People who don't get turned around easily.

People who don't mistake one tree for another.

And yet the land around them behaves like it has its own rules — rules that humans only occasionally notice.

2. The Boulder That Appeared Overnight

One of the most unsettling accounts comes from a pair of paddlers camping on a small peninsula on the North Arm. When they set up their tents, they remembered the clearing perfectly:

- flat moss
- open understory
- a long-dead log lying to the east
- and an unobstructed view of the water

The next morning, a boulder the size of a refrigerator sat fifteen feet from their tent door.

Not rolled. Not dragged. Not weathered.

An enormous piece of stone that *should have made noise* getting there.

Except neither paddler heard anything.

One of them said:

"This wasn't a small rock. You'd need machinery to move something that size. And it was right beside our tent."

They walked around the clearing in disbelief. No drag marks. No uprooted moss. No disturbed soil.

The paddler repeated the same phrase three times during our interview:

"It wasn't there. It just wasn't."

This is the type of moment where the forest reveals a disturbing truth:

It does not operate within the same physical consistency we expect.

3. The Shape of a Shoreline That Changes Without Warning

Fog plays tricks on anyone — but fog does not change geography.

A woman from Ottawa was paddling solo in late September. Heavy morning fog covered the lake. She approached a familiar shoreline she had camped on the year before — a stretch she knew intimately: a sloping granite shelf lined with old storm-felled pines.

But when she arrived, the shoreline was wrong.

Not slightly wrong.Completely wrong.

Instead of granite, she found:

- a sandy crescent
- dense brush
- no pines
- no slope
- no familiar features

She marked the spot on her map again.It was the correct location.

She waited in the fog for twenty minutes.

When it lifted, the shoreline was back to normal.

The granite.The fallen pines.The slope.Everything she remembered.

She stared at it for a long time, unable to understand what she'd seen earlier.

Her voice trembled as she told me:

"The fog didn't hide the shoreline. It replaced it."

4. The Cabin That Was There — Then Gone

This incident happened on the southeast side of Lake Temagami. A pair of teenagers on an overnight trip claimed they saw a small abandoned cabin tucked along the treeline — boarded windows, slanted roof, moss-covered siding.

They paddled past it, pointed at it, discussed exploring it.

But the next day they paddled the same route back…

…and the cabin was gone.

The shoreline was untouched:

- no clearing
- no foundation
- no disturbed brush
- no signs a structure had ever existed

When the teenagers told their parents, the parents chalked it up to imagination.

Years later, one of the boys — now a grown man — still insisted:

"We both saw it. We talked about it for at least ten minutes. That cabin was real."

And he's not the only one.Floating structures.Phantom docks.Cabins that appear once and never again.

Temagami has dozens of such accounts — and they all share one chilling trait:

Witnesses see structures where structures cannot possibly be.

5. The Ridge That Shifted in the Night

A bush pilot stationed in the region for years told me a story he'd rarely shared.

He'd landed near a remote lake north of Obabika. He camped at the base of a narrow ridge, about thirty meters tall and sharply defined. He noted its shape carefully — pilots do that instinctively, making mental maps of the land.

He slept lightly.

When he woke early before sunrise and stepped out to relieve himself, he felt an odd disorientation.

Something was wrong.

It took him several minutes to realize it was the ridge.

It had shifted.

Not dramatically — perhaps twenty or thirty feet farther to the left. But enough that the treeline on top now aligned differently.

He checked his bearings. He walked around the camp. He re-measured distances.

The land had moved.

Or he had. But only while asleep.

He told me:

"Ridges don't move. But that one did."

He never camped in that area again.

6. When Portage Trails Rebuild Themselves

Several groups have described the same unnerving phenomenon:

a portage that looks different every time they use it — even on the same trip.

A guide told me about a trail near the Florence Lake system. On the way in, it was:

- rocky
- narrow
- heavily rooted

On the way out, two days later, the same trail appeared:

- wider
- flatter
- straighter

He wasn't mistaken. He had marked a broken tree limb earlier — and on the way out, the limb was still broken but now stood beside a section of trail that seemed almost… newly formed.

He said:

"It was like the forest pressed a reset button."

Trails don't "rebuild themselves." Yet enough people have experienced it to place it firmly in the pattern.

7. The Tree That Appeared in Front of the Tent

A father camping with his young daughter near Diamond Lake woke at 3 a.m. to relieve himself. The moonlight gave everything a faint silver outline.

He stepped out of the tent and froze.

A tree — a young spruce, maybe six or seven feet tall — stood directly in front of the tent entrance.

He insisted it wasn't there earlier.He'd cleared the site carefully.He remembered every stump, every root, every rock.

But now a tree stood there.Healthy.Rooted.Integrated into the forest floor.

No drag marks.No loose soil.No disturbance around it.

He touched it — half expecting it to dissolve or wobble.

It was real.

He woke his daughter at dawn.By then, the tree was gone.

Not cut.Not fallen.

Just… gone.

He told me:

"It didn't grow. It didn't move. It was placed."

Placed by what, he didn't want to guess.

8. When Distance Stretches and Shrinks

Trail distortion is common. But distance distortion is stranger.

Witnesses frequently describe:

- portages that feel twice as long as they should
- trails that abruptly shorten
- lakes that take an hour to paddle across one day and twenty minutes the next
- hills that seem taller or smaller than memory

Two brothers hiked a familiar trail near Temagami Island that normally takes 45 minutes.

It took 2 hours. But their pace never slowed.

The next day, the same trail took 35 minutes.

Same gear. Same weather. Same men.

This pattern almost always coexists with:

- sightings
- auditory signals
- feelings of being watched

The distortion isn't severe — it never puts people in immediate danger.

It's gentle.

Almost like the land is subtly shifting around you, but only just enough for you to notice.

9. The Forest "Breathing" — A Witness Description I'll Never Forget

A woman from Thunder Bay described something so strange I didn't know what to make of it.

She said that during a solo hike near Anima Nipissing, she felt the forest expand and contract.

Not physically — not in a dramatic way — but perceptually, like the size of the world around her changed for a moment.

She said:

"It felt like the woods exhaled.

And when it inhaled, everything was different."

The trees seemed farther apart.Then closer.The sky seemed wider.Then narrower.

She wasn't panicked.She wasn't dehydrated.She wasn't inexperienced.

She simply observed something no human should ever feel:

a landscape subtly shifting, as if alive.

10. Are These Shifts Caused by the Beings?

This is the core question.

Do the creatures move through the land in a way that influences perception? Or does the land itself contain anomalies that the creatures use?

Three possibilities appear again:

1. The beings use trails and terrain humans cannot perceive.

They move through the "true" version of the forest — not the human one.

2. The beings manipulate their environment subtly.

Not magically — but biologically or behaviorally in a way we don't understand.

3. The land is layered.

And humans occasionally slip into a layer normally occupied by the beings.

One hunter summed it up better than I ever could:

"They don't hide from us.

We walk into the wrong version of the forest and they're already there."

11. What This Chapter Reveals About the Larger Mystery

This chapter isn't about fantasy.It's about **consistency** — a pattern of strange environmental distortion witnessed by credible people.

Taken individually:

- a misplaced tree
- a shifted ridge
- a vanished cabin
- a portage that changes length

These could be misinterpretations.

But together?

Across decades?

Across hundreds of witnesses?

Across overlapping hotspots?

A truth emerges:

**Temagami is not simply a wilderness.

It is a dynamic, shifting landscape where physical reality bends around the presence of something else.**

Not always dramatically.Not always dangerously.But undeniably.

The beings are part of it. The land is part of it. And humans walk between those two forces without realizing it.

CHAPTER 9 — VANISHINGS AND NEAR-MISSES

How People Slip Out of Sight in the Temagami Wilderness — and Why Some Return Without Knowing Where They've Been

1. The Disappearances No One Talks About Publicly

When someone goes missing in Temagami, it rarely makes the news. You might hear about a search on the radio, or see a brief mention on a local bulletin board, but the details never capture what really matters — how the disappearances actually happen.

People don't wander off trails because they're careless. They don't vanish because they're underprepared. Most of these people are:

- hunters
- paddlers
- lifelong woodsmen
- experienced hikers
- campers who know how to navigate

And yet they go missing in ways that don't fit normal wilderness logic.

Sometimes for hours. Sometimes for days. Sometimes permanently.

And the survivors — the ones who come back — tell stories that don't line up with the terrain, the timelines, or their memories.

They talk about:

- **sound vanishing**
- **trails that dissolve underfoot**
- **time missing in blocks**
- **a thick stillness that feels wrong**
- **being watched from behind trees**
- **hearing someone call their name who wasn't there**

These vanishings aren't accidents.They're part of the same pattern we've been building toward.

The land rearranges.Time slips.The watchers observe.

And sometimes people walk into the wrong part of the forest — the part not meant for them.

2. The Boy Who Walked Away Mid-Sentence

One of the earliest stories came from a couple camping with their teenage son on a small peninsula off Diamond Lake.

The father told me:

"He was walking six feet in front of us, talking about the stars.

He finished a sentence — and then he wasn't there."

Not ran.Not wandered.Not turned a corner.

Gone.

The parents froze.They called his name.They ran forward, expecting to see him just out of sight.

But the trail was empty.Silent.No footsteps.No broken branches.No crash through brush.

Nothing.

They called for him for twenty minutes before running back to camp and grabbing headlamps.

He reappeared seventy minutes later — walking out of the trees on the opposite side of the peninsula.

Disoriented.Confused.Calm.

He told them he'd been walking the entire time.

Except the terrain where he came from was impassable — sheer roots and thick undergrowth that no human could move through without sound or struggle.

The boy's memory was clean:

"I walked straight. That's all I remember.

I thought you were behind me."

That single line still bothers me:

He didn't realize he had vanished.

3. The Canoeist Who Lost Two Hours and Forty Feet

A man from Brantford described a moment that lasted seconds — for him — and nearly three hours for his partner.

They were paddling along a quiet channel in early evening, planning to camp. He leaned over to splash water on his face and felt a strange heaviness, like the air thickened around him.

When he looked up, the light was wrong.

It wasn't late evening anymore.It was dusk.

His partner was yelling his name from the shore.

He paddled over, confused.She'd been searching for him for almost three hours — convinced he'd drowned.

He insisted:

"I was right here. I never moved."

The distance between them was small.Maybe forty feet of open water.

But for three hours he was invisible to her.

No splash.No voice.No silhouette.

Only when he lifted his head again did he "reappear."

His partner said it best:

"He didn't return.

He just… showed up where he already was."

4. The Hunter Who Walked in Circles — But Left No Circles Behind

A Temagami-area hunter described an incident where he became lost for most of a morning — despite walking a perfectly straight line.

He'd followed a fresh deer track through a mixed stand of birch and white pine. He checked his compass constantly. He knew exactly where he was.

Until he stepped into a low clearing and found his own bootprints.

Not similar ones.His.

He crouched down.Checked the prints.Confirmed the tread pattern.

He had walked in a circle.

Except the forest around him was wrong:

- no landmarks he recognized
- undergrowth he hadn't passed through
- a ridge that should have been on his left now on his right

He looked up.

A tall, unmoving figure stood between two pines about eighty yards away.

He blinked.The figure was gone.

He ran.

When he finally reached a familiar logging road, TWO HOURS had passed.

But his GPS track — recorded automatically — showed him walking in a straight line the entire time.

No arc. No circle. No loop.

Just a line.

He said:

"Something moved around me, not the other way around."

5. The Girl Who Vanished at the Campsite Edge

One of the darkest near-misses happened on a summer youth trip.

A 14-year-old girl stepped away from the group to wash her hands in the lake only fifteen feet from camp. Two leaders watched her walk to the water.

They turned to speak to the rest of the group — just seconds.

When they turned back, she was gone.

The lake was calm. No splash. No scream. No footprints along the wet sand. No sign of a fall.

Just absence.

Searchers combed the area for hours before finding her at dusk — sitting upright at the base of a cedar nearly a kilometer inland.

Her hands were dry. Her feet were clean. There were no scratches on her legs.

But she was crying.

She told her rescuers:

"I took one step and the lake disappeared."

She remembered nothing after that.

Nothing except a "buzzing" in her ears and a sense of "too many trees."

6. The Three Canoes That Split Into Two Worlds

One of the strangest cases involved three canoes traveling together on a long crossing. The lake was calm. The paddlers were experienced. They kept an even formation.

In the lead canoe were two men who regularly tripped in Temagami.

In the second canoe were a father and his adult daughter.

In the third canoe were two friends.

At some point during the crossing, the middle canoe simply... drifted out of sight.

The lead canoe stopped and waited. The third canoe closed the distance.

But the middle canoe — the one they had been traveling next to only minutes earlier — was gone.

Not behind an island. Not in a fog bank.

Gone.

The father and daughter reappeared at a campsite two hours later — visibly shaken — insisting they had paddled straight the whole time and had seen no one.

One of the men from the lead canoe said:

"They were ten feet off our stern.

Then they were somewhere else. Not ahead. Not behind. Somewhere else."

The father said:

"We never stopped paddling. But the lake changed around us."

7. The Man Who Was Found Standing Still

In the early 2000s, searchers found a missing hiker standing upright in a clearing near a marsh. He responded when spoken to, but his eyes were "hollow," as if he were sleepwalking.

He had been missing for 14 hours.

He told rescuers:

"I kept walking.

But the world wouldn't let me out."

What he meant by that was unclear. But he remembered:

- paths that ended abruptly
- sounds that echoed strangely
- a feeling of being watched
- a figure pacing beside him in the trees

He also described seeing his own footprints vanish behind him as he walked.

He said:

"Every time I looked back, the forest erased where I'd been."

He had no injuries. No dehydration. No trauma.

But he could not remember a single transition — only moments, disconnected like mismatched tiles.

8. The Missing Man Whose Gear Was Untouched

In one of the coldest cases I reviewed, a man solo-tripping near the Kokoko area disappeared without a trace.

His canoe was found tied properly to a tree. His tent was zipped. His food barrel untouched. His pack leaned against the firepit exactly as he always left it.

Everything was orderly.

No signs of struggle.No animal activity.No overturned equipment.

It was as if he had stepped out of his gear and simply evaporated.

Searchers found faint impressions in a patch of moss — but they didn't match human stride.

Too far apart.Too deep.Too deliberate.

A tracker told me:

"Those weren't his.

And they weren't bear."

The man was never found.

9. The Sound That Lures People Away

Another pattern emerges in these accounts:**many disappearances begin with sound.**

Not fearful sound.Not threatening sound.

Familiar sound.

People describe:

- hearing their name called
- hearing a friend's voice
- hearing a whistle they recognize

- hearing something that sounds like a child laughing

One camper said:

"I heard my brother call me from the trees.

My brother was 100 kilometers away."

A young man who disappeared for six hours later told rescuers:

"I followed a voice.

It sounded exactly like my girlfriend."

Several people describe hearing:

- soft footsteps
- murmured voices
- someone clearing their throat
- a dog whining
- someone crying

But no one is there.

It pulls them off-trail. Toward something. Away from safety.

These are the same mimicry patterns described near sightings of tall figures.

Coincidence? Or something else?

10. Why These Vanishings Don't Fit Normal Explanations

If you strip the fear out of these stories and analyze them clinically, you get anomalies that survival experts cannot easily explain:

- people disappearing mid-step
- lost individuals reappearing without injuries
- missing time with no memory gaps
- footprints that go nowhere
- trails that rearrange
- groups splitting into different "versions" of the same route
- voices that imitate loved ones
- sightings before or after disappearances
- time dilation or compression
- electronics failing

This isn't typical lost-person behavior. This is environmental distortion.

Something interacting with:

- perception
- direction
- time

- awareness
- memory
- physical presence

And always — always — in the same handful of hotspot regions.

11. What These Stories Say About the Larger Mystery

Taken individually, these vanishings and near-misses could be dismissed as rare wilderness accidents.

But woven together, they form a pattern too consistent to ignore:

People don't just get lost in Temagami.

They get pulled.**

People don't just wander off trails.

The trails change around them.**

People don't just disappear.

They step — unknowingly — into places that don't always let them go.**

And whatever these beings are…

Whatever intelligence watches from the ridges…

Whatever signals echo through the trees…

They don't merely live in Temagami.

They shape it.

And sometimes —briefly —they pull people into their version of the forest.

CHAPTER 10 — WINDLESS WHISPERS

Voices, Murmurs, and Communication That Doesn't Travel Through Air the Way It Should

1. When the Air Is Perfectly Still — But Something Speaks Anyway

There's a sound you don't expect to hear deep in the Temagami backcountry.

A whisper.

Not a gust through pine needles.Not a breeze dragging across the lake.Not the sigh of branches bending under their own weight.

A real whisper.

A voice too soft to be a shout, too clear to be imagination, and too close to be an echo.

These whispers don't behave like normal sound.They don't ride wind currents.They don't bend with branches.They don't repeat or echo or fade naturally the way forest sound usually does.

They appear in:

- dead calm
- humid silence
- heavy fog

- perfectly still air
- thick forest pockets where even wind refuses to travel

Most witnesses described the same feeling:

"I heard something — but the air wasn't moving."

If the land in earlier chapters rearranges itself physically, the whispers rearrange something else:

Your sense of safety. Your sense of distance. Your sense of reality.

These whispers are not aggressive. They're not out to terrify. They simply… appear.

And they carry a chilling consistency across decades.

2. The Whisper That Traveled Through Still Air

A Temagami ranger I spoke with remembered a moment near the Sharp Rock area that never left him.

He was checking fire risk conditions, the sun high and the lake mirror-still. No wind. No chop. No movement in the trees.

He stood on a narrow peninsula writing notes when he heard a whisper behind him.

Just one breath of sound:

"hey."

He spun around. No one. Not even a squirrel.

He listened carefully.

The air remained absolutely still.

He told me:

"Whispers travel with wind. But there wasn't any. The air was heavy as syrup."

He dismissed it as imagination — until it happened again.

This time the whisper came from his left.

"**hey.**"Soft.Almost curious.

He felt something then — not fear, but the awareness of being observed.

A full ten seconds passed.

Then the third whisper came from ten feet behind him, far too close for comfort.

He left immediately.

He said:

"It wasn't trying to scare me.

It just wanted me to know I wasn't alone."

3. The Hunting Camp That Heard a Murmur in the Earth

One hunter described hearing whispers that didn't move through air at all —they moved through ground.

He was walking a small ridge early in the morning when he felt a vibration in the soil. Subtle. Almost like a low hum. He stopped, thinking it was distant machinery.

But then he heard it —a murmur, low and conversational.

Not a single voice. More like two or three overlapping in soft tones.

He crouched and placed his hand on the ground.

The vibration grew stronger.

He stood up and backed away. The moment his boots left the ridge, the whispering stopped completely.

His partner, waiting at the camp, confirmed something else:

While the hunter had been gone, the partner heard something circling the tent — slow, bipedal footsteps, too heavy to be human.

The hunter told me:

"It didn't feel like the ground was talking.

It felt like something beneath it was."

4. The Whisper That Called a Camper's Name — When No One Was Awake

One of the most credible accounts came from a woman camping with her teenage niece. The girl fell asleep early, exhausted from a long portage day. The woman stayed awake to stoke the fire and enjoy the coals.

Around midnight, as the wind died and the forest settled, she heard her niece whisper her name:

"Auntie?"

Soft. Almost sleep-like.

She turned toward the tent and said, softly:

"What is it?"

No answer.

She got up and looked inside.

The girl was fast asleep.

She stepped back out, confused. As she stood by the fire, she heard the whisper again — this time from the treeline.

"Auntie."

Same voice. Same tone. Same inflection.

She backed away from the trees, instinctively holding her breath. The air was perfectly still. Not even the smallest breeze touched her skin.

She told me:

"I recognized the voice.

But it wasn't her. It wasn't even human, not exactly. It was like someone recreating her voice from memory."

She didn't sleep that night.

5. The Whisper Beside the Tent That Wasn't a Voice at All

Some whispers aren't voices.They're... something else.

A man from Sudbury described a whisper that sounded more like **syllables without meaning**, spoken in a rhythm that felt almost conversational.

He was lying awake in his sleeping bag when he heard it:

A soft string of sounds, no louder than breath:

"tsha... sheh... tasha... she..."

Right outside the tent wall.

Not mumbling.Not wind.Not animal sound.

Language — but no language he recognized.

He froze.

He could hear the articulation — lips shaping syllables, air passing through a throat.But the sound was far too close to be natural, hovering inches from the nylon.

Then it stopped.

A moment later, footsteps circled the tent — slow, deliberate, heavy.

Not a bear.Not a moose.

Two-legged.Measured.Aware.

As the footsteps faded, he heard one final whisper near the back of the tent:

"sha…"

He told me:

"If it wanted to attack me, it would have.

It wasn't here to scare me.

It was communicating — just not with me."

That detail matters.

These whispers rarely feel directed at the witness.

They feel like someone speaking *near* you or *through* you but not *to* you.

6. The Portage Whispers That Moved Faster Than Human Footsteps

A group of paddlers was halfway along a long portage near the Wakimika Triangle when they heard whispering close behind them.

They turned — nothing.

They walked again.

The whispering resumed — a soft multi-toned murmur, like several people speaking quietly.

They stopped again. Silence.

They walked.

The whispering moved ahead of them now — not behind.

Then to the right. Then the left. Then a hundred meters ahead.

The sound darted around them with unnatural speed:

- close
- then distant
- then overhead
- then along the ground

Not echo. Not wind. Not acoustics.

Something was moving faster than human footsteps — but staying just out of sight.

The leader of the group said:

"It felt like we were being discussed."

7. The Whisper That Came From Inside the Cabin Wall

One of the creepiest accounts came from a man wintering in a small trapper's cabin in the Lady Evelyn area.

He slept on a bunk pushed against a log wall. Around 2 a.m., he woke to the sound of whispering.

Not in the room.Not outside.

Inside the wall.

He pressed his ear to the logs and heard a faint, steady murmur — too muffled to understand,too rhythmic to be random.

He thought it was wind through a crack —until the whispering stopped the moment he lifted his ear.

He tested it repeatedly.

Ear against the wall — whisper.Ear off — silence.

Nothing alive could fit in that wall.No rodent is that quiet, that articulate, or that coordinated.

The man told me:

"I don't know if it was the forest or something in it.

But it wasn't human."

He moved his bunk the next night.

He didn't sleep.

8. These Are Not Just "Voices" — They Are *Communication*

When you compile these accounts, a pattern appears:

The whispers are not random.They're part of the same communication network that includes:

- knocks
- whistles
- pacing
- drumming
- mimicry
- forest silence
- trail distortion

It's not one phenomenon. It's one *system*.

And whispers are the closest thing to a direct interface with that system.

Whispers happen:

- before sightings
- after sightings
- in places where time slips
- in places where trails shift
- where the land rearranges
- near large footprints
- near pacing events
- in hotspots with multiple reports

They occur in clusters — not isolated incidents.

They accompany presence.

Not threat.

Not violence.

Presence.

9. Why These Whispers Cannot Be Natural

Skeptics always ask:

Couldn't whispers be:

- wind?
- animals?
- acoustics?
- human voices carrying from far away?

Here's why the answer is no:

1. They occur in total windless stillness.

No breeze.No movement in the canopy.

2. Animals do not whisper in human cadence.

Not even close.

**3. Voices traveling long distances distort.

These whispers do not.**

4. They move too fast and too directionally.

Sound doesn't relocate instantly.

5. Multiple witnesses hear the exact same whisper from different directions.

6. Many occur beside tents — inches from fabric.

7. They change location, tone, and distance unnaturally.

There is intelligence behind them —whether animal, humanoid, or something else.

10. What This Chapter Reveals About the Temagami Mystery

This chapter deepens the pattern we've been building:

- The land rearranges.
- Time slips.
- Trails distort.
- Figures watch from ridges.
- Footsteps pace camps.
- Voices call names.

- Whispers move through still air.

Taken together, these are not random wilderness strangenesses.

They represent a system of **communication**, **presence**, and **observation** that operates just beyond human perception.

Humans are not the only ones navigating Temagami.

Something else is there. Something that speaks softly when the wind refuses to move. Something that does not need breath or distance to carry its voice.

And whatever it is — the whispers are only the beginning.

CHAPTER 11 — THE SILENT ONES
The Beings Who Move Without Sound, Slip Between Trees, and Vanish the Moment You Realize They're There

1. When Movement Makes No Sound at All

Every creature in Temagami makes noise.

A squirrel darts through brush like a wind-up toy.A rabbit snaps twigs underfoot as it flees.A moose crashes through branches like a falling refrigerator.Even black bears — despite their reputation for sneakiness — cannot cross the forest floor without revealing themselves.

But for decades, people in Temagami have described something else entirely:

movement with no sound. Not reduced sound.Not muffled sound.Zero sound.

Something large — heavier than a man, taller than a man — gliding through brush without disturbing a leaf.

Hunters say it best:

"Everything makes noise up here. Except them."

"Them" being the Silent Ones —the beings who move as if gravity doesn't apply in the same way it does to the rest of the forest.

These sightings are not dramatic.They don't involve threats or chases.

They begin with a flicker of motion.A shadow between trees.A shift in light.

And then the disturbing realization:

You didn't hear it move.

Not a snap.Not a step.Not a breath.Not a single displaced twig.

Nothing.

2. The Hunter Near Red Squirrel Who Saw Something Step Behind a Tree

This account came from a hunter who'd been tracking deer near Red Squirrel Road for most of his life.

He was sitting on a low ridge when he saw movement out of the corner of his eye.

A tall, dark shape — upright — stepping behind a pine.

He turned his head in time to see the final portion of the movement:a broad back, long arm, and massive torso slipping behind the trunk.

He waited for the sound.

Branches snapping.Ground shifting.Brush parting.

Nothing.

He walked toward the tree slowly, rifle lowered, expecting to see the creature on the other side.

But the ground was undisturbed.No tracks.No compressed leaf litter.No broken twigs.

He told me:

"A moose can't vanish.

A bear can't move silently.

And a person couldn't disappear that fast.

But whatever I saw did."

What unsettled him most wasn't the disappearance.

It was the silence behind the movement — the void where sound should have been.

3. The Two Campers Who Watched a Figure Cross the Shoreline Without Stirring the Water

Two friends camped along a quiet bay near Obabika Lake woke at dawn to a glass-calm shoreline. One of them stepped out of the tent to relieve himself and froze in place.

A tall figure was walking along the granite edge across the bay.Striding.Smooth.Effortless.

He called his friend quietly.They both watched.

The figure moved with a long, deliberate gait —the way a tall human might walk with purpose.

But it left no prints.No disturbance in the morning dew on the rock.No change in the reflected water.

The witness described it like this:

"It moved across wet granite without sliding.

Like it weighed nothing."

They watched it step behind a small outcrop —

—and it never reappeared on the other side.

The second witness added:

"It didn't run.

It didn't hide.

It just stepped out of the world."

4. The Silent Figures Seen From Canoes at Dusk

Canoeists often see more than hikers do — especially at dusk when the shoreline is backlit and every silhouette becomes sharper.

Several paddlers have described:

- tall, dark shapes
- standing perfectly still on shore

- then stepping back into the forest
- without a single sound

One man said he watched a figure take three long steps up a steep incline:

"If I took those steps, I'd slip.

It climbed like it wasn't touching the ground."

No crumbling moss.No falling rock.No labored motion.

Just smooth, impossible quiet.

These encounters often end with the figure vanishing in a way no large animal can —not by running,not by ducking,but by blending into shadow and becoming indistinguishable from the forest behind it.

As if it belongs to the shade more than the land.

5. The Woman Who Saw a Figure Run Across a Clearing Without Making a Sound

This account came from a woman who worked as an outdoor educator near Temagami Island.

She woke before her group to gather water. Near the shoreline was a small grassy clearing. As she turned to head back toward camp, she saw a tall dark figure sprint across the open ground.

She described it as:

- upright
- long-legged
- shockingly fast

But here's the detail that chilled her most:

"Grass makes noise.

Even dew makes noise.

But this thing was completely silent."

She said the only sound she heard was her own breathing.

The figure reached the treeline and dissolved into the shadows.

She told me:

"I know what running sounds like.

This wasn't running.

This was motion without consequence."

She never reported it officially, worried about putting her job at risk.

But she never forgot it.

6. The Black Shape at the Edge of the Tent

Some of the most unnerving Silent One encounters happen within feet of a tent.

A man camping alone near Florence Lake woke to the feeling that something was outside.

No sound.No footsteps.Just awareness.

He sat up slowly, heart pounding, and looked through the mesh.

A tall, black shape stood twenty feet away.

Perfectly still.Broad.Unmoving.

He watched it for nearly thirty seconds before it turned — one smooth, soundless motion — and stepped behind a spruce.

No footfall.No brush movement.No snap of branches.

Just absence.

He didn't sleep again that night.

He told me:

"It wasn't trying to get closer.

It was checking on something.

I don't know if that something was me."

7. The Disturbing Consistency: They Move as if the Ground Doesn't Matter

Across all these encounters, a pattern becomes unmistakable:

These beings move as if they exist slightly outside the rules of physical space.

Witnesses describe:

- no sound
- no disturbance of ground cover
- no snapping branches
- no displaced water
- no weight impact
- no visible exertion

Not running silently —but running without affecting the environment at all.

Not walking softly —but walking as if gravity works differently for them.

One hunter put it bluntly:

"It was like watching a ghost made of muscle."

Another said:

"It moved wrong.

Not unnaturally —

just… outside our idea of natural."

8. Are the Silent Ones the Same as the Watchers?

There's overlap between the Watchers (the standing, observing figures) and the Silent Ones (those that move).

But many witnesses insist the Silent Ones are different.

Here's how they describe the differences:

The Watchers

- Always still
- Always distant
- Always observing
- Heavily built
- Often huge

The Silent Ones

- Move quickly
- Move soundlessly
- Thinner, but still tall
- Fade into shadow
- Appear only briefly
- Behave with purpose

It's possible these are:

- different ages
- different sexes
- different castes in a species
- different types of beings altogether

Or —the same being behaving in two distinct modes:

Observe quietly.Approach silently.

Either way, the difference matters.

Especially because the Silent Ones appear more physically present —more willing to approachmore willing to movemore connected to the shifting trails, time loss, and vanishings described in earlier chapters.

9. When Silence Is a Warning

One of the strangest consistent details in these encounters is this:

Witnesses say they felt a sudden void in sound before the Silent Ones appeared.

Birds vanish.Wind ceases.Insects stop.Forest noise drops instantly to zero.

Not a slow quieting.A snap.

A sudden absence.Like someone muted the world.

This silence isn't peaceful.

It's charged.

And every person who experienced it said the same thing:

"Something was coming."

Or more unsettling:

"Something was already there."

10. What This Chapter Reveals About the Larger Mystery

So far in this book, we've described:

- watchers on ridges
- mimicry in the trees
- shifting trails
- missing time
- vanishings
- whispers
- signals

The Silent Ones are the physical manifestation of all those patterns—the beings that move through the landscape with the fluidity of shadow and the presence of flesh.

They are not spirits. Not hallucinations. Not tricks of light.

They are real. They are witnessed. They are consistent.

And they are **perfectly adapted to a forest that shifts around them**.

If the watchers are the sentinels, and the whispers are the communication, and the trail distortions are the environment reacting,

the Silent Ones are the ones who navigate between all those forces with effortless precision.

CHAPTER 12 — TRACKS THAT SHOULD NOT EXIST
The Footprints Too Large, Too Deep, and Too Intelligent to Belong to Any Known Animal in the Temagami Wilderness

1. Footprints That Tell a Story No One Wants to Believe

In the Temagami wilderness, you learn early on that the ground is honest.

Animals lie. People misremember. Voices echo. Shadows trick the eyes.

But the earth? The earth records.

Every step. Every weight shift. Every stride. Every direction change.

And when something leaves a 17-inch footprint in perfect mud, the earth is saying something that human logic isn't comfortable with.

Witnesses don't lead with excitement when they describe these prints. They lead with discomfort.

"It was too big."

"Too human."

"Too heavy."

"Too deep."

"Too wrong."

Because the moment you see a print like that, the world becomes larger and stranger than you thought. And nothing you've learned about bears, moose, humans, or predators helps you make sense of it.

What these prints show — clearly, consistently, repeatedly — is this:

Something huge, bipedal, and intelligent is moving through Temagami.

And no one knows what.

2. The 18-Inch Print on the Shore of Obabika

One of the clearest tracks was found by a pair of paddlers landing on Obabika's northern shoreline to filter water.

The woman stepped onto a patch of mud and froze. She backed away slowly.

Her partner stepped forward to look.

There, pressed deeply into the dark mud, was a footprint as long as her forearm:

- **18 inches from heel to toe**
- **7 inches wide at the ball of the foot**
- **clear mid-foot flexion**

- **five distinct toes**
- **deepest at the midline, not the heel**

A bear print? Impossible. Bears don't show mid-foot flexibility. Bears show claws.

A moose? Moose don't have toes.

A human? A human would have to be eight to ten feet tall — and barefoot — in mid-spring water temperatures.

The woman said:

"It wasn't an impression. It was a stamp.

Something incredibly heavy stepped there, and it wasn't human."

They followed the trackway along the shore for about twenty meters.

Then the tracks walked onto granite —

— and vanished.

No scuffs. No dirt transfer. No further prints.

The creature knew exactly where to stop leaving evidence.

3. The Tracks in the Snow That Stopped at a Tree

Winter tracks provide some of the strongest evidence because snow reveals weight and direction clearly. But winter tracks also produce the strangest endings.

A trapper near the Lady Evelyn River found a set of prints in fresh snow:

- enormous
- spaced far apart
- perfectly straight gait
- deep enough to indicate something extremely heavy

He followed them for nearly half a kilometer.

Then he reached a cedar.

The tracks walked right up to the base of the tree —and stopped.

No return prints.No diverted trail.No side tracks.No prints on the other side.

As if the creature simply stepped into the tree.

Or vanished.

The trapper told me:

"I'm not saying it teleported.

I'm saying it didn't walk away the way it walked in."

This pattern shows up in dozens of winter reports:

Tracks that begin and end cleanly in places no creature could disappear.

No collapsing snow.No disturbed bark.No branch snapping.

Just an ending.

4. The Three-Toed Tracks on a Frozen Bog

Not all prints in Temagami are human-like. Some are stranger.

A group of ice fishers found a set of three-toed tracks crossing a frozen bog south of Temagami Island.

The prints were:

- about 12 inches long
- deeply pressed into the snow
- three wide toes ending in slightly pointed tips
- a heel pad oval and disproportionately large

A wolverine? No. Too large.

A bear partially stepping? No. Three toes are too clear, and the spacing wrong.

A bird? Absolutely not. No bird on earth weighs enough to sink ten centimeters into the snow.

One of the fishers said:

"It looked like a dinosaur walked across that bog."

The stride was long — nearly five feet between prints.

Whatever made it didn't slip, didn't drag, didn't lose balance.

It walked as confidently as a human on dry land.

And like many trackways in Temagami, it ended at a line of tamaracks with no return route.

5. The Tracks Beside the Cabin — and the Window Smudge

A cabin owner near the North Arm returned after several weeks away to find large prints in the snow circling the building.

He described them as:

- roughly 16 inches long
- human-shaped
- heavily pressed into the snow
- spaced about six feet apart

But the strangest part wasn't the prints.

It was the smudge.

On the outside of his front window, about seven feet off the ground, was a long horizontal smear. As if something broad-chested had leaned in to look through the glass.

Not a handprint. Not a nose print. Just a dark, rough smudge at a height no human could easily reach.

He said:

"Whatever it was wanted to see inside."

A bear might sniff a window. A human might lean in.

But neither leaves a 7-foot-high smudge while walking on two legs around the house.

6. The Stride Length That Defies Human Anatomy

Many trackways show a feature impossible for humans to replicate naturally:

stride.

Normal human stride:2.5 to 3 feet.

Tall human maximum stride:4 to 4.5 feet.

Bigfoot-type stride in Temagami:**6, 7, even 8 feet per step.**

One hunter tried to replicate a trackway near Sharp Rock Inlet. He placed his boots in the prints as best he could and tried to walk in the same rhythm.

He failed instantly.

He said:

"I couldn't even do one step without pulling a groin muscle."

He measured the trackway:

- 17-inch prints
- 7.5-foot stride
- perfectly straight gait

- no dragging
- no side step
- complete confidence of movement

No modern athlete could reproduce those steps in the woods.

Not quietly.Not cleanly.Not at night.Not over rough terrain.

But something can.

7. The Tracks That Sink Far Too Deep

Weight tells a story.

A black bear weighing 400 pounds leaves a very specific depth in mud or snow.

A moose weighing 800 pounds leaves even deeper tracks — and typically destroys the surrounding vegetation.

But many of Temagami's anomalous tracks sink far deeper than either animal would.

Some tracks press 6–8 inches into hard-packed ground.

A retired geologist from Sudbury used soil density readings to estimate weight based on track depth.

His conservative estimate?

750–900 pounds.

But the stride — long, upright, balanced — does not match anything that heavy except a human-shaped figure.

He said:

"If a moose weighed that much, the forest floor would collapse under it.

But these prints were elegant — not destructive."

The weight-to-grace ratio is one of the most perplexing elements:

Too heavy to be human.Too quiet to be animal.Too consistent to be mistake.

8. The Double-Print Phenomenon: Two Beings, Two Sizes

Multiple trackways show something unnerving:

a large set of prints…and a smaller set beside them.

Not children's prints.Not human prints.Not bear cub prints.

Smaller hominid-shaped prints.Still large by human standards — 11–14 inches — but noticeably smaller than the primary trackway.

One winter hiker found:

- 19-inch prints (adult?)
- 13-inch prints (juvenile?)

Walking side-by-side along a logging road.

The smaller prints occasionally stepped inside the larger ones — almost as if following or mimicking.

A pattern also found in many Bigfoot reports in the Pacific Northwest.

The hiker said:

"It looked like a parent teaching a child how to walk quietly."

The trackway eventually left the road and cut into dense spruce where snow made it impossible to follow.

But the parallel prints tell a story:

whatever these beings are, they travel in groups —and they teach each other.

9. The Tracks That Show Intentional Avoidance of Detection

Several witnesses note something strange:

trackways often appear only in the places where the ground *must* show prints.

For example:

A paddler found prints along a muddy shoreline, but none in the sand 30 feet earlier where a creature would have walked.

Another found perfect prints in soft moss — but none in harder soil just ahead.

A trapper found prints on a patch of melted snow — but none on the deeper snow that surrounded it.

It's as if the creature:

- avoids fragile areas
- chooses where to step
- knows how to minimize evidence
- places feet deliberately

And that's not speculation — it's consistent across dozens of cases.

One ranger said:

"These prints weren't mistakes. They were exceptions."

Which implies intelligence.And a desire not to be found.

10. What These Tracks Reveal About the Larger Mystery

After compiling all these accounts — and analyzing them for consistency, environmental conditions, and anatomical logic — a clear pattern emerges.

Temagami's anomalous tracks show:

- **an upright, bipedal walker**
- **massive size and weight**
- **incredible silence of movement**
- **long stride length**
- **clear foot morphology**

- **absence of claws**
- **mid-foot flexibility**
- **intentional avoidance of soft ground**
- **occasional multi-individual trackways**
- **trackways that begin and end impossibly**

This isn't misidentification.

This isn't hoaxing —you cannot fake hundreds of pounds of pressure in perfect vertical compression.

This is something real.

Something that leaves physical evidence.Something with anatomy.Something that walks like a humanbut is far larger and far more adapted to moving through shifting terrain.

The beings from the previous chapters — the watchers, the silent ones, the whisperers — now have a physical footprint.

Literally.

CHAPTER 13 — THE CABIN PACER
The Being That Circles Camps at Night — Slow, Deliberate, and Without Fear of Human Presence

1. When Something Walks Around Your Shelter in the Middle of the Night

Anyone who has spent enough nights in the backcountry will eventually hear something moving outside the tent.

A curious raccoon. A sniffing deer. A heavy-footed bear.

These are normal.

Predictable.

They make sense.

But there is a different kind of visitor — a visitor whose presence is unmistakably deliberate.

Not a shuffle. Not a foraging animal. Not a single pass through camp.

Something that **walks around your shelter** slowly, methodically, with long, heavy bipedal strides — and seems to be studying what's inside.

People call it different things:

- "the night walker"
- "the circler"

- "the observer"
- "the midnight pair of feet"
- "the cabin pacer"

But everyone describes the same feeling:

It's not curious.It's evaluating.

This being doesn't come to steal food.It doesn't come to attack.

It comes to **assess.**

2. The Family Who Heard It Circle Their Cabin at 3 A.M.

A family staying at a small cabin near Temagami Island woke to the sound of heavy footsteps outside.

Not bear footsteps —those are uneven, shifting, weight-distributing.

These were **bipedal**:

- a steady cadence
- heel-first impact
- pacing back and forth along the wall
- turning at sharp angles no quadruped makes

The father whispered to his wife:

"Someone's out there."

He grabbed the flashlight and moved toward the window — careful not to step loudly.

As he approached, he heard the footsteps shift to the rear of the cabin.

He hurried to the back window.

Nothing.

He moved to the side window.

Still nothing.

But the footsteps continued —clearly audible, right outside —even though no visible shape was there.

He pressed his ear to the log wall and felt faint vibration through the wood.

Something large.Heavy.Deliberate.

After ten minutes, the pacing stopped.

Not faded.Stopped.

The family didn't sleep for the rest of the night.

In the morning, they found fresh impressions in the moss:

- bipedal
- spaced far apart
- heel-to-toe

- roughly 15–17 inches long

The father said:

"It wasn't a bear.

It walked like a person.

A very big person."

3. The Miner's Cabin That Was Circled for Three Nights Straight

A former miner working in the area north of Lady Evelyn described a week he never forgot.

He stayed in a remote logging cabin — old, drafty, with a tin roof and a loose door latch.

The first night, around midnight, he heard slow, heavy steps outside.

He assumed it was a moose.Until he heard the **rhythm**.

Step.Step.Step.

A long pause.

Step.Step.

Approaching the cabin from the left side.Stopping.Shifting weight.Then continuing around the back.

The pacing lasted nearly twenty minutes.

On the second night, it returned — but this time it stayed longer.

He lay still in bed, rifle propped beside him, listening to the rhythmic movement.

Step.Crunch.Step.

Slow.Measured.In control.

On the third night, the pacing happened earlier — just after dusk.

Right outside the door.

He watched the shadow of the figure block the firelight coming from the woodstove through the small window.

A huge, tall outline.

Too broad to be human.

He told me:

"It wasn't scared of me.

It knew I was alone.

And it was deciding something."

On the fourth night — nothing.

It never returned.

He left the cabin early and never stayed there again.

4. The Pacer Outside a Tent at Florence Lake

A pair of hikers set up camp near Florence Lake on a cool September evening. They were experienced, calm, and not easily spooked.

Around 1 AM, the sound of footsteps woke both of them.

They froze.

The steps were heavy —too heavy for a deer.

And they were upright —a clear, steady two-beat rhythm.

Step…Step…Step…

Moving in a circle around their tent.

The woman whispered:

"That's not a bear."

He agreed.

Whatever it was, it was tall.

They could hear the breath pattern —slow, deep exhales above the height of the tent.

At one point, it paused directly beside the head of the tent. They could feel the presence. Not heat — but **mass**.

A living weight just feet away.

After nearly fifteen minutes, the footsteps moved toward the treeline.

Then came a final, heavy step —as if the creature shifted its stance to listen.

Total silence followed.

One of the hikers said:

"It knew we were awake.

And it didn't care."

5. The Pacer Who Knocked on the Cabin Wall

A story passed around locals describes a trapper's cabin deep near the Makobe River.

The man staying there heard pacing often — but one winter night, it changed.

Instead of circles, instead of slow steps, he heard **knuckles** strike the log wall.

Three times.

Not a grab. Not a claw. Not an animal.

A knock.

THUD. THUD. THUD.

Then pacing resumed again.

He grabbed his rifle and didn't move from the bunk.

At dawn, he stepped outside and found:

- humanoid tracks

- enormous stride length
- a smooth trail around the cabin
- handprints on the frosted exterior logs

Not bear pads.Not claw marks.

Handprints.

Wide palms.Thick fingers.No gloves.

He told me:

"It wasn't curious.

It was letting me know it knew I was there."

6. Why the Pacing Feels Intelligent

Several details separate the Cabin Pacer from any known animal behavior:

1. Repeated passes around human structures

Animals don't circle cabins deliberately.

People do.

2. Pauses at windows

Witnesses report hearing the footsteps stop exactly at window height.

3. Inspection behavior

The pacing often slows near:

- doors
- vents
- water barrels
- tents
- backpacks

As if studying.

4. Rarely disturbs equipment

It is not looking for food. Not rummaging. Not foraging.

The Pacer is not hungry.

The Pacer is aware.

5. Returns in the same nightly pattern

Some cabins experience pacing for nights in a row, at the **same exact time.**

Predators don't keep schedules.

But something intelligent might.

7. The Night Pacer at Fox Lake — and the Missing Print

A group of anglers heard pacing around their cabin on Fox Lake for two nights. Heavy. Bipedal. Slow.

On the third night, something reached up and **rattled the rain gutter**.

Not ripped. Just tested.

In the morning, they found a single massive footprint beside the cabin — but only one.

Perfectly pressed into the ground.

No incoming prints. No outgoing prints. Just the single track.

One man said:

"It left a calling card.

That's worse than leaving a trail."

He burned the boot mat where the print had partially transferred.

8. The Cabin Pacer and the Silent Ones: Are They Linked?

Several patterns suggest the Pacer is not a separate entity, but a **behavior** of the same beings described earlier:

- tall, upright figures
- massive stride
- no fear of humans

- perfect silence when needed
- intelligent decision-making
- ability to move without leaving obvious tracks

The watchers stay distant. The silent ones approach. The whisperers communicate.

But the Cabin Pacer performs the most unnerving role: **direct surveillance.**

It is the only behavior pattern that places these beings **deliberately within feet of sleeping humans** with no fear of consequences.

They are not looking for food.

They are observing.

Evaluating.

Perhaps learning.

9. Why the Cabin Pacer Is One of the Most Important Clues

If you analyze wildlife behavior, the Pacer makes no sense.

But if you analyze **intelligence**, the Pacer becomes the clearest evidence of it:

- choosing the perimeter
- maintaining distance

- staying silent
- inspecting
- returning at scheduled times
- leaving minimal evidence
- avoiding confrontation
- circling like a guard or sentry

This is **patterned behavior**.

This is **organized behavior**.

This is **purposeful behavior**.

The Cabin Pacer shows us that whatever is moving through Temagami:

- understands humans
- understands structures
- understands boundaries
- evaluates without engaging
- comes close without harm
- is confident enough to approach silently

Something smart is watching us sleep.

10. What This Chapter Reveals About the Larger Mystery

The Cabin Pacer ties together everything we know so far:

- the watchers on the ridges
- the silent ones in the trees
- the trackways with impossible stride
- the whispers in still air
- the vanishings
- the time slips
- the shifting trails

This chapter reveals their **behavior pattern.**

These beings do not stay deep in the forest.

They come to us.

They come to our doors. Our windows. Our tents. Our cabins. Our shelters.

Not hunting.

Not attacking.

Watching.

Studying us up close.

The deeper we go into Temagami, the more we learn:

We are the ones being researched.

CHAPTER 14 — THE LAKE CREATURES

Huge Shapes Beneath Canoes, Silent Swimmers in Blackwater, and the Ancient Animals Witnesses Swear Don't Match Anything Known in Ontario

1. The Water Holds Secrets the Forest Cannot Hide

People think of Temagami as a land of tall pines and endless ridges — but the lakes define this place far more than the trees.

Hundreds of lakes. Thousands of back bays. Blackwater gullies deeper than anything in southern Ontario. Cold, silent trenches where sunlight disappears.

The water is clear near shore, but turn toward the depths and it becomes a mirror for dark shapes you don't want to see.

And that's the thing about Temagami's lakes:

You don't always see what's below you — but you *feel* it.

A quiet shift under the canoe. A slow roll of displaced water. A shadow darker than the bottom. A presence swimming in the deep.

When witnesses talk about the lake creatures, they never sound excited.

They sound unsettled.

They say things like:

"It was too big."

"It was under us for too long."

"It followed the canoe."

"No fish moves like that."

Whatever moves under Temagami is not a single species, not a myth, and not imagination.

It's a pattern —and far older than any hominid sightings.

2. The Shape That Followed a Canoe on Rabbit Lake

A pair of brothers paddling across Rabbit Lake late in the evening felt something thump lightly beneath the canoe — not a rock, not a log. Something soft, but massive.

They looked down and saw a long, dark shape rising just beneath the hull.

Not a pike.Not a lake trout.

Something *wide*, moving slowly, with a shadow that extended beyond the canoe's length.

One of the brothers said:

"It looked like the back of a submarine."

The shape didn't bump them again.

Instead, it drifted beneath their canoe for nearly thirty seconds — close enough that they could see a faint outline through the dark water.

Then it peeled away and disappeared into the depths.

The older brother said:

"It knew we were there.

It followed us on purpose."

3. The Fishermen Who Saw a Head Rise Behind the Boat

Two men trolling near the mouth of Sharp Rock Inlet were anchored for the evening. The water was calm. The sky was a low dark blue.

Without warning, one of them felt the boat shift. Not from wind — there was none. Not from waves — the lake was flat.

He looked behind the stern and saw a head rise from the water.

Not a beaver. Not an otter.

A head the size of a volleyball —dark, smooth, and round. Too large for any known animal in the region.

It rose silently, looked in their direction, then slipped beneath the surface without a splash.

The second man described it:

"No wake. No bubbles.

It just... dropped."

When they cut the motor and listened, they heard a soft swirling noise beneath the boat —as if something circled once, then descended.

Neither of them fished that bay again.

4. The Canoeist Who Felt Something Push from Below

A solo paddler was crossing a deep channel between Temagami Island and Bear Island when the canoe rose several inches as if lifted from beneath.

He braced himself, thinking he had hit submerged timber.

But then the canoe **tilted** —slightly, deliberately —as if something huge pressed upward and rolled beneath him.

He looked down and saw nothing but blackwater —yet the canoe rocked again, harder this time.

He said:

"It wasn't wind.

It wasn't waves.

Something was under me."

The pressure stopped just as suddenly.

He paddled fast until he reached shore.

That night he couldn't shake the feeling that he'd paddled over something that was choosing to stay unseen.

5. The Group Who Saw Something as Long as Their Canoe

While exploring a narrow interior lake near Diamond, a group of friends saw a dark, eel-like shape glide beneath them.

The water was clear, so they could see the entire silhouette:

- long,
- sinuous,
- thicker than a man's torso,
- moving in a smooth S-pattern like an anaconda underwater.

One friend shouted:

"What the hell is that?"

The shape coiled once in shallow water and then shot into deeper water too quickly for any local fish.

They paddled to shore immediately.

One of them later said:

"It moved like a snake, but it was way too big.

And snakes don't live in this lake."

The shadow they described fits no known species in Ontario — no fish, no reptile, no mammal.

Just… something else.

6. The Night Something Surfaced Beside a Campsite

A pair of campers on High Rock Island heard heavy water displacement late at night. Not splashy movement — slow, intentional rising.

They grabbed a flashlight and pointed it toward the lake.

What they saw was a dark hump about four feet across, rising silently ten meters from shore.

It wasn't a loon. Wasn't a beaver. Wasn't human.

The hump lifted slightly, turned in their direction, then dipped again as if sinking vertically. No splashing, no turbulence.

One camper said:

"It was like watching a huge, slow swimmer take one breath and go back under."

They didn't sleep after that.

7. The Creature That Slid Past a Dock Without a Sound

On a quiet July evening, a family staying at a rental cabin heard the dock ropes creaking gently — as if something large passed underneath.

The father shone a flashlight.

In the beam, they saw a pale grey movement under the water:

- long,
- smooth-bodied,
- with a slow, muscular ripple,
- at least twelve feet from head to tail,
- moving purposefully along the dock's edge.

The mother said:

"It had the mass of a big fish,

but the movement of something that knows where it's going."

She described the back as "dull grey, like wet stone."

It slid out of the light and vanished deeper than the beam could reach.

8. Fish Don't Act Like This — So What Does?

When you list Temagami's known aquatic species, nothing matches the descriptions above:

- lake trout max out at 40–50 inches
- pike rarely exceed 45 inches
- sturgeon don't inhabit most inland lakes
- otters don't move like serpents
- beavers don't disappear silently into deep water
- loons leave wakes
- snapping turtles cannot glide that fast

The behaviors people describe are:

- coordinated
- intelligent
- silent
- curious
- unafraid
- often enormous

And they appear in lakes:

- too deep for easy exploration
- with underwater caves
- with abandoned mine shafts
- with sheer drop-offs

- with cold, oxygen-rich pockets where strange life can thrive

Some local theories include:

- an unknown eel species
- a remnant prehistoric fish
- large amphibians
- some type of aquatic mammal
- something related to hominid sightings
- or something older
- deeper
- more adapted to the blackwater worldthan anything we understand.

But none of these theories fit all the accounts.

Because it isn't just size.It's the *behavior*.

These creatures observe canoes.Shadow boats.Follow paddlers.Surface silently.And vanish with no turbulence at all.

Animals don't do that.

Predators do that.

Or something with predator-level intelligence.

9. The Oldest Stories: "The Deep Ones"

Temagami's First Nation elders have old accounts —not always shared widely —of creatures in the deepest lakes that are not fish, not snakes, not mammals.

They describe:

- long-bodied lake dwellers
- silent swimmers
- beings that travel beneath the surface without breaking it
- things that rarely harm, but always watch
- creatures that move between lakes through underground channels

Some call them:

"the ones beneath."

Others describe them simply as:

"the long shadows."

One elderly man told me:

"The land has its beings.

The water has its own.

Don't confuse the two."

He said the lake creatures are older than the hominid beings. Older than the forests. Older than the islands.

And they do not fear boats.

They study boats.

10. What the Lake Creatures Reveal About the Larger Mystery

This chapter deepens the scope of the entire investigation.

The Temagami mystery is not confined to:

- the watchers on the ridges
- the silent ones in the forest
- the pacers around cabins
- the mimic voices
- the vanishings
- the shifting trails
- the time loss

It extends below the surface.

To depths humans rarely consider. To a world colder, darker, and less explored than the forest floor.

The presence beneath Temagami's lakes is not a myth or a single species —it's a recurring pattern across decades of witness accounts.

These beings are not random anomalies.

They form a hidden ecosystem.A second layer of the unexplained.A deeper chapter in Temagami's true wilderness.

And whatever exists down there:

- swims silently
- moves with intention
- observes from below
- and is aware of us

CHAPTER 15 — WOLVES THAT STAND TOO TALL

Massive Canids, Upright Shadows, and the Dogman-Like Creatures Witnesses Encounter in the Deep Temagami Backcountry

1. When a Wolf Stops Looking Like a Wolf

Wolves are part of Temagami's identity. They move through the region's forests like ghosts — silent, efficient, and rarely seen up close. Experienced woodsmen hardly fear them. Wolves avoid humans. Always have.

But some reports from Temagami describe something very different.

Not normal wolves. Not coywolves. Not hybrids.

Something **larger**. Something **stranger**. Something that seems to know when someone is watching.

People describe:

- wolves taller than a man's shoulder
- animals walking upright on two legs
- canid heads peering from behind trees
- silhouettes that shift between quadrupedal and bipedal movement

- heavy, loud footsteps not consistent with any known wolf
- eyes that reflect not yellow or green — but **red**

These aren't werewolves.They aren't movie monsters.They aren't folklore.

They're patterns.

Patterns described by trappers, campers, hunters, paddlers, and locals who know exactly what a real wolf looks like.

What they're seeing isn't that.

2. The Hunter Who Saw a Wolf Standing Upright on a Ridge

A hunter near the North Arm recounts a moment that still makes him uncomfortable to speak about.

He was glassing a distant ridge for moose when he saw movement — a dark, canid-shaped silhouette stepping between two pines. From afar, he assumed it was a large wolf.

But then it stood fully upright.

Not on a log.Not reaching for food.Not jumping.

Standing. Upright.Like a man.

Broad shoulders.Long forelimbs hanging naturally.A head shaped exactly like a wolf's — ears pointed, muzzle long, proportions correct.

He froze, unsure of what he was looking at.

Then the creature turned its head.

It saw him.

Even from hundreds of yards away, he felt the weight of its attention.

He said:

"Wolves don't do that.

Whatever it was, it knew I was watching —

and it stood there anyway."

After several long seconds, it dropped back to all fours and trotted along the ridge.

Not awkwardly.Smoothly.Effortlessly.

Like a creature completely familiar with both positions.

3. The Night Something Circled a Tent Snarling on Two Legs

Two campers at a remote lake off the Temagami River experienced something far more direct.

They were drifting into sleep when they heard footsteps — heavy ones — circling their tent.

Not four steps.Two.

Bipedal.

Then came a deep, low growl — right beside the nylon.

Not the guttural "huff" of a bear. Not the throaty rumble of a large dog. Something deeper. Something closer to a wolf's growl pushed through a chest the size of a black bear's.

The campers froze.

The creature moved again —**long, deliberate steps**— circling the tent as if inspecting it.

One camper whispered:

"That's walking.

Wolves don't walk like that."

At one point, the creature stopped directly behind the tent. They could hear breath — loud, heavy, canid breath — above the height of the tent's spine.

Then a single tap — like something pressing a claw against the fabric.

The creature moved away slowly, the growl fading into the distance.

They didn't unzip the tent until sunrise.

4. The Wolf Too Large to Be a Wolf

A snowmobiler near Temagami Station in late winter saw something at the tree line that he first assumed was a wolf.

It stood broadside. Massive. Thick coat. Huge chest.

But the proportions were wrong. Far too tall. Shoulders too high. Neck too long.

As he slowed the sled to look, the animal turned toward him.

It was enormous —taller than any timber wolf, heavier than a German shepherd, with a stance too level to be a bear.

The head was unmistakably canid.

But the body was… stretched. Elongated. Predatory in a way wolf physiology doesn't allow.

When he revved the engine, the creature didn't run.

Instead, it took **three strides** — effortless, gliding strides — and disappeared into dense bush.

He told me:

"If that was a wolf, it was the biggest wolf I've ever heard of.

But wolves don't move like that.

It was too smooth. Too fast. Too tall."

5. The Creature Seen Crossing a Portage on Two Legs

Two paddlers near Wakimika Lake were finishing a portage when they saw something up ahead crossing the trail.

At first, they thought it was a large man in dark clothing.

But then the "man" leaned forward and dropped to all fours —in a fluid, unnatural motion —and loped into the woods with the stride of a wolf.

The transition was too smooth to be human. Too balanced to be a bear. Too coordinated to be a person crawling.

One paddler said:

"It was like watching something switch bodies.

One second, it looked human.

The next, it moved like an animal."

They dropped their packs and waited nearly twenty minutes before continuing.

Whatever they saw wasn't spooked. It simply didn't care.

6. The Red-Eyed Canid on the Shoreline

A man camping solo on a small island in Red Squirrel Lake woke in the early morning to the sound of something drinking at the shoreline.

He stepped out with a headlamp.

A massive canid stood at the water's edge — far too large to be a wolf.

When the beam hit its eyes, he expected the typical yellow or green reflection.

Instead, the eyes shone **bright red** —not glowing, but reflecting red light in a way that suggested different retinal structure.

The creature lifted its head slowly, stared at him for several seconds, and then walked up the shoreline on two legs before dropping to all fours and disappearing.

He said:

"No wolf does that.

And no human looks like that."

7. Tracks That Don't Match Any Known Canid

Several trackways attributed to these creatures have been found:

- canid-shaped pads
- claw marks
- elongated toes
- enormous size
- stride lengths up to six feet

But some show something more disturbing:

the creature switching from four tracks to two — mid-trail.

One trapper found a trail like this near Temagami Island:

- four-pawed canid tracks for 30 meters
- then suddenly bipedal human-like prints,

- then back to four-pawed

The spacing on the two-legged portion was massive — nearly the stride of the hominid tracks described in earlier chapters.

He told me:

"I've tracked wolves for 40 years.

Wolves don't do that.

Whatever it was, it was comfortable on two feet."

8. Are These Wolves? Hybrids? A Mutation? Or Something Else?

Biologists point out that wolves can occasionally "stand," but never walk bipedally. Never stride naturally. Never transition smoothly.

And certainly never reach the height or mass described in these encounters.

Some locals believe these are:

- oversized wolves
- rare genetic anomalies
- massive coywolf hybrids
- misinterpreted bears

But each of those explanations crumbles under the weight of the reports.

Because the people making these reports aren't inexperienced hikers.

They're hunters.Paddlers.Trappers.Bushcrafters.Locals who know the difference between:

- bears standing
- wolves walking
- coyotes loping
- a person in dark clothing

These are not misidentifications.

9. The Dogman Theory — And Why It Matters Less Than People Think

The so-called "Dogman" phenomenon exists in folklore across North America, but Temagami's reports don't fully match the classic descriptions.

Witnesses here describe:

- a creature with full canid anatomy
- comfortable on two legs
- capable on four
- huge, wolf-like proportions
- intelligent behavior

- predatory movement
- minimal fear
- silent stalking
- shadow-like transitions

This isn't a shapeshifter or a supernatural monster.

This is a **physical animal** with a biology that doesn't match anything officially recognized in Ontario.

The exact classification doesn't matter.

What matters is that multiple people have encountered canid predators that:

stand too tall, move too smoothly, and behave too intelligently to be normal wolves.

10. What These Creatures Mean for the Larger Temagami Mystery

The wolves-that-aren't-wolves add another dimension to everything we've uncovered so far:

- tall hominid figures
- silent ones
- watchers
- pacers

- lake creatures
- vanishings
- whisperers
- time distortions
- shifting trails

Each phenomenon overlaps without fully matching the others.

But these canid-like creatures are different because:

they behave like apex predators.They assess.They stalk.They test.They do not flee.

They also appear in the same corridors where hominid sightings peak.

Which raises a chilling possibility:

Temagami may not have one unknown species.It may have an entire ecosystem of them.

Different beings.Different roles.Different behaviors.

Some watch.Some stalk.Some pace.Some whisper.Some swim.Some walk upright at the treeline with eyes that reflect red in the night.

Each one adds another piece to the map.

CHAPTER 16 — THE CLOAKED PRESENCES

Entities That Bend Light, Appear as Distortions, and Move Through the Forest Without a Body You Can Fully See

1. Seeing Something That Isn't Exactly Visible

Some encounters in Temagami don't involve large silhouettes, clear tracks, or anything tangibly physical.

They involve **the absence of something** —or the distortion of something that should be there.

People describe:

- a shimmer like heat rising off pavement
- a clear outline of something tall that bends light
- a shape you only see through your peripheral vision
- something walking without a body
- a density in the air that moves with intent
- motion where no animal or person is visible

Witnesses often struggle to put the experience into words.

They say things like:

"I saw something, but I couldn't see it."

"It had shape — but not a body."

"It was like looking at reality glitch for a second."

"Something walked between the trees, but I only saw the space it displaced."

These aren't ghost stories. These aren't hallucinations. They're consistent wilderness encounters across decades — reported by hunters, paddlers, trappers, search personnel, and locals.

And in many cases, the beings described here appear in the **exact same regions** as the watchers, the silent ones, and the pacing entities.

It's as if these "cloaked presences" are part of the same system — but exist half a step out of phase with our reality.

2. The Shimmering Figure on the Portage Trail

A group of three paddlers were halfway down a long portage when the lead man stopped abruptly.

He whispered:

"Something's ahead of us."

The others saw nothing at first — until the lead paddler stepped to the left, adjusting his angle of view. Then they all saw it:

A tall, upright distortion standing between two jack pines.

The shape wasn't opaque. It wasn't shadow. It wasn't reflective.

It was a **shimmer** — like the air above a hot road, except concentrated into a humanoid outline.

Six feet tall. Maybe more. Broad. Still.

They froze, watching in disbelief.

Then the shape moved — smoothly, silently — to the right, bending the background behind it as it passed.

The forest returned to normal once it vanished.

One of the paddlers said:

"It wasn't invisible.

It was wrong. Like reality bent around it."

Afterward, the group continued the portage without speaking.

3. The Trail Camera That Captured "Nothing" Moving

A cabin owner near the Makobe River set up a trail cam after repeated pacing around his property.

For two weeks, the camera captured:

- deer
- fox
- raccoons

- a black bear

But on the third weekend, the camera triggered multiple times during a twelve-minute window —and each photo showed the same thing:

Empty forest, but the trees behind were slightly warped in a vertical line.

Every shot had the distortion in a different place:

- between two cedars
- crossing a clearing
- near the woodpile
- beside the cabin wall

The man showed the sequence to two friends, all experienced outdoorsmen.

Their reactions were identical:

"Something walked through the frame."

A biologist he later consulted suggested a sun flare or heat distortion.

Except it was night.And the temperature was near freezing.

Something was there.The camera just didn't know how to capture it.

4. The Shape That Blocked the Stars

A lone paddler on Maple Mountain Lake lay in his sleeping bag outside, watching the stars.

It was a clear night.Still air.Perfect visibility.

Then, without wind or warning, the stars above him went dark — not all at once, but in a **moving line**, as if something tall passed between him and the sky.

He sat upright as the line of darkness slid silently past the top of his field of vision.

He saw no body.No animal.No figure.

Just **stars vanishing and reappearing**, as if blocked by something invisible.

He later said:

"It was like a giant passed over me, but you could only see the outline by the stars it hid."

He didn't sleep outside again.

5. The Hunter Who Saw Footsteps Without Legs

A Temagami hunter tracked a deer well before sunrise. He moved slowly, carefully, listening to the forest.

Then he heard footsteps —not behind him,but to his right.

Slow, heavy steps on dry leaves.

He turned his headlamp toward the soundand saw…nothing.

But the footsteps continued.

Then he noticed the leaves shifting in a line —as if something invisible was walking through them, pressing them down with weight.

The leaf litter depressed in time with each step.

He whispered to himself:

"What the hell?"

Then the steps accelerated —and the leaf impressions became deeper, like someone running.

He didn't pursue the deer after that.

He went straight back to his truck.

6. The Presence That Reflected in the Lake But Had No Body

A pair of paddlers at dusk noticed something strange on the water —a ripple pattern moving across the lake without any visible cause.

It wasn't wind-driven. The rest of the lake was glass.

It wasn't a fish. The movement was too linear, too wide.

Then one woman pointed to the reflection:

"There — do you see it?"

In the water, they saw the faint outline of something tall moving along the shoreline.

Not the actual being — but its **reflection**.

Like a humanoid distortion standing near the trees. But when they turned to look directly at the shore, nothing was there.

Only the reflection revealed it.

Whatever it was, it stood for long moments, then shifted and moved deeper into the woods.

The paddlers sat in silence, terrified to move.

7. Cloaked… or Something Else?

Witnesses use words like:

- cloaked
- camouflaged
- transparent
- blended
- phased
- glitching
- warped
- shimmered

But most admit they're guessing — because what they saw doesn't fit any natural phenomenon.

Some theories include:

1. Optical camouflage

The way cephalopods change color — but on a massive, upright creature.

2. Light-bending fur or skin

Like a biological invisibility cloak.

3. A perceptual anomaly

The creature is solid, but our eyes cannot render it properly.

4. Partial interdimensional presence

Not supernatural — simply a form of existence that overlaps ours irregularly.

5. A being evolved specifically to avoid detection

Master-level predator camouflage.

But none of these theories fully account for:

- reflections showing what eyes cannot
- trail cameras capturing warped outlines
- footsteps producing physical ground impressions
- the same shapes appearing near hominid sightings

- the ability to move without sound

Something physical is present.Something intelligent.Something adapted to remain unseen.

Whatever the Silent Ones are,whatever the watchers are,these cloaked entities are likely connected.

Perhaps:

the watchers observe,the pacers investigate,and the cloaked ones move between them unseen.

8. Are These the Same Beings as the Silent Ones?

It's possible the cloaked presences are simply a stealth behavior of the same beings.

The Silent Ones:

- appear physically
- move without sound
- leave tracks
- reveal themselves occasionally

The Cloaked Presences:

- rarely show full form
- distort the environment

- leave imperfect visual impressions
- are sensed more than seen

Multiple witnesses have described a cloaked presence immediately before or after a clear hominid sighting.

It may be the same creature, switching between visibility states.

Or these entities may be:

- juveniles
- scouts
- a separate predatory species
- or something older than the hominids

In any case, people in Temagami have repeatedly seen beings who are not fully visible — but are fully aware.

9. What the Cloaked Presences Mean for the Larger Mystery

So far, we've established:

- watchers on ridges
- silent ones gliding through trees
- wolf-like predators
- lake creatures
- pacing entities

- mimicry
- vanishings
- footprints
- time slips
- trail distortions

The cloaked presences add a new dimension:

perception manipulation.

These beings don't just hide physically.

They hide from *sight itself*.

This means:

- the forest may be more populated with unknown life than we realize
- these entities may observe humans far more often than we detect
- sightings represent rare *failures* of their camouflage
- their presence explains pacing without seeing a body
- they may be the source of whisper-like distortions
- their existence connects vanishings to perception
- they may predictably occupy trail corridors and ridge lines

The deeper the pattern goes, the more it becomes clear:

Temagami is not empty wilderness. It is controlled wilderness.

By beings that move faster, quieter, and more invisibly than anything officially recognized by science.

CHAPTER 17 — THE NIGHT VISITORS
The Beings Who Approach Tents, Touch Walls, and Stand Inches from Sleeping Campers in the Temagami Backcountry

1. When Something Stands Where No Animal Should Be

There's a specific kind of fear you only learn in the backcountry — the fear that wakes you from dead sleep and tells you:

You are not alone.

Not the fear of a bear nosing around.Not the fear of wind shifting your tarp.Not the fear of a raccoon rummaging through camp.

This fear is old.Instinctual.Something your ancestors would have recognized instantly:

"Something is standing right outside."

Witnesses across Temagami describe the same experience:

- a sudden awareness in the middle of the night
- footsteps too heavy for deer
- breath too deep for any known animal
- silence too deliberate to be chance

- and a presence too large to ignore

You lie there, frozen in your sleeping bag, every sense straining for details —

And then it touches the tent.

Sometimes softly. Sometimes with weight. Sometimes with curiosity.

Never with violence.

But always with intent.

2. The Handprint on the Tent at Red Squirrel Lake

Two brothers camping on Red Squirrel Lake in late August went to bed after a calm and uneventful day.

Around 3 a.m., the older brother awoke to the faintest rustling outside. Not movement —just… awareness.

He lay still, listening.

Then the nylon beside his head pressed inward —a clear imprint of a hand.

Not a paw. Not a branch.

A **hand.**

Five thick fingers. Wide palm. Heavy pressure. Held there for three slow seconds.

He slapped his younger brother awake. The handprint slid upward, dragging slightly across the tent wall before lifting away.

The younger brother whispered:

"That was a person."

But when they worked up the courage to look outside at dawn, they found no footprints — only two depressions in the moss exactly where something large would have been kneeling or standing.

A bear wouldn't make a handprint. And no human barefoot in the forest would stand with that much confidence inches from sleeping strangers.

The older brother said:

"It wasn't trying to get in.

It was trying to understand who was inside."

That distinction matters.

3. The Visitor Who Pressed Its Face Against the Tent Mesh

A young couple canoeing north of Turner Lake set up camp on a small pine-covered point. They fell asleep after watching embers glow in the firepit.

Around midnight, the woman woke to a strange pressure against the tent wall. Soft at first. Then firmer. Like something pushing its weight down.

She opened her eyes.

A face was pressed to the mesh.

Not a human face.Not a bear's snout.

A broad, dark shape with pronounced brow ridges and deep-set eyes —too far apart to be human,too forward-facing to be a bear,too large to be anything she could understand.

It held still for several seconds.Breathing slow.Steady.

She couldn't scream.She couldn't move.

Her partner woke and whispered:

"What is that?"

As soon as he spoke, the visitor stepped back —upright, silent — and its shadow moved across the tent wall before vanishing into the trees.

They packed before sunrise and didn't speak of it for months.

4. The Being That Leaned on a Cabin Door

A man staying in a remote cabin near Rabbitnose Lake heard slow, dragging footsteps on the porch.He assumed it was a bear,until he heard something heavy lean against the door.

Not scratching.Not sniffing.

Leaning.

Pressing weight deliberately on the wood,as if testing the structure.

The doorframe creaked under the pressure.

He grabbed his rifle —not to shoot but to brace himself for whatever was out there.

For nearly thirty seconds, the weight remained against the door.

Then it lifted.

A single, heavy step thudded against the porch. Another.

Then silence.

In the morning, he found a massive partial footprint on the porch —nearly 16 inches long —and a long smear of dirt and moisture across the door.

He said:

"It wasn't trying to break in.

It was listening."

5. The Visitors Who Tap Tents

One of the strangest patterns is what campers call "the tapping."

It's never aggressive. Never frantic.

Always controlled.

A single tap. Sometimes two.

Always on the opposite side of where people are lying.

Witnesses describe:

- a long finger dragging lightly
- a single knuckle tap
- a slow push
- a gentle poke
- a brush across the roof
- a press that holds just long enough to be unmistakable

One group near Maple Mountain counted *seven* distinct taps over the course of an hour — each spaced fifteen to twenty minutes apartas if something was pacing the treesand occasionally reaching out to announce its return.

One man whispered to me:

"They weren't curious about the gear.

They were curious about us."

6. The Presence That Pulled on the Guy Lines

A solo camper near Obabika woke to the unmistakable sensation of his tent being **pulled.**

Not blown.Pulled.

The guy line tightened sharply — once — as if something had grabbed it and given a short, testing tug.

He sat upright, heart hammering.

Then another line pulled. On the opposite end of the tent.

Something was walking around the tent, testing the tension points with deliberate, intelligent evaluation.

He whispered:

"Whatever it was, it knew what it was doing."

He stayed still until dawn.

When he stepped outside, the ground was too compact for prints — but all four guy lines had faint dust smears where something large had touched them.

7. The Visitors Who Watch the Fire Die

Multiple groups describe the same scenario:

- the fire crackles low
- voices around the campsite soften
- the night grows cold
- the forest falls silent
- something approaches quietly from the treeline

It never comes while flames are strong.

Only when embers remain.

A group near Ferguson Bay described seeing a tall silhouette step out from behind the birches at the moment their fire collapsed inward.

Not approaching aggressively —standing at the edge of the orange glow.

Watching.

When one of them lifted a lantern, the figure turned and melted into the trees without sound.

One man said:

"It walked in on purpose,

and it left on purpose.

It was waiting for the fire to die."

8. Why These Visitors Never Attack

It's important to understand:

None of these encounters involve violence.

No ripped tents.No forced entries.No physical harm.

The Night Visitors do not behave like predators.

They behave like **observers**:

- slow
- patient
- curious
- deliberate

- unafraid
- intelligent
- assessing

They do not:

- steal food
- destroy gear
- cause panic intentionally

They come closeonly long enough to understandwho is in their territory.

One experienced Temagami paddler told me:

"It wasn't hunting.

It was learning."

That statement captures the tone of every Night Visitor encounter.

9. Are These the Same Beings as the Cabin Pacer and the Silent Ones?

There is overwhelming consistency among all three behaviors:

- upright posture
- massive chest and shoulders
- heavy bipedal stride

- ability to move silently when desired
- no fear of humans
- curiosity about camps
- intelligence beyond animal instinct
- extreme precision in proximity

The watchers remain at a distance.The silent ones move with supernatural quiet.The pacers inspect territory.The night visitors approach closest of all.

They are almost certainly the same beings —or closely related variants.

The only difference is **distance.**

The Night Visitors cross the boundary:

They enter the space where humans sleep.

Close enough to touch canvas.Close enough to breathe inches away.Close enough to study.

10. What the Night Visitors Reveal About the Larger Mystery

Hominid sightingsfootprintstrail distortionstime losslake creatureswolves-that-aren't-wolvescloaked presences

— these all establish something unknown in the Temagami wilderness.

But the Night Visitors show something else:

These beings are not avoiding us. They are actively engaging.

Not violently. Not maliciously.

Just… intimately.

They want to understand humans. They want to observe us at our most vulnerable. They come only at night, when the forest is silent and the fire is low. And they leave with the confidence of something that knows:

We cannot stop them from coming close.

CHAPTER 18 — THE NIGHT THE FOREST TURNED AGAINST THEM (as reported to me)
Two Researchers, One Cabin, and a Night That Didn't Go as Planned

1. Why They Returned

I wasn't there the night it happened.

At the time, I was working on a film out of town — long days, late nights, the kind of schedule that pushes your fieldwork onto the back burner whether you like it or not. But two researchers I trust — Mark and Jensen — had room in their schedule and decided to head into the Lady Evelyn region on their own.

Their goal was straightforward: revisit the 2009 cabin sighting site.

It was one of the few Temagami encounters that included **photographs** — grainy, low-light images capturing a tall, upright figure between two cedars behind a small cabin. The photos had been circulated quietly among researchers for years.

The couple who took them never returned. They sold the cabin. They left the region. Their final email to researchers was brief:

"We won't go back. You shouldn't either. Something followed us that night."

That email was already a decade old by the time Mark and Jensen headed in.

They weren't expecting anything to still be there.

None of us were.

2. Following a Decade-Old Email

The directions weren't perfect. They'd been forwarded so many times the formatting was broken, the landmarks described vaguely, and they had no GPS coordinates. But Mark and Jensen eventually found **one** cabin that matched:

- the slope
- the cedar stand
- the porch angle
- the clearing pattern
- and the tree alignment visible in the 2009 photos

They approached it once in the afternoon — strictly to confirm no one was there and that the structure matched the photos. The place was empty.

Then they backed out and didn't go near the cabin again.

Standard field practice. You verify. You retreat. You observe from distance.

3. Camped Legally on Crown Land

They found a flat stretch of crown land five or six minutes away as the crow flies — legal, secluded, and far enough that they couldn't see the cabin through the trees anymore.

The forest swallowed it completely.

Even though the cabin was out of sight, both of them later said the same thing:

"We always knew which direction it was in."

Some sites have a pressure to them — a psychic weight, almost — that doesn't lift just because you break line of sight.

By dusk, they had gear set, the parabolic mic angled toward the ridge, and the EMF meter logging small, irregular spikes.

Nothing dramatic.Just enough to make them pay attention.

4. The Forest Tightens

According to their notes, the air felt "compressed" before the sun even set."Like the silence was expecting something," Mark wrote.

The usual dusk chorus never came. No thrushes, no nightjars, not even the distant call of loons across the lake.

The forest acted as one organism.One that had noticed new variables in its territory.

They weren't afraid.But they were alert.

Good researchers know that "stillness" is often the first anomaly.

5. The First Knock

At 9:16 p.m., a deep **THUNK** echoed through the trees.

Not a casual branch-drop.Not a woodpecker.Not an accident.

A purposeful knock.

Jensen later said it felt like "someone hitting the wall of a barn with a baseball bat."

A second knock followed.Closer.Heavier.

Then silence so complete it made both men sit frozen.

The forest was waiting for their answer.

They didn't give one.

6. The Pacing Begins

Around 10 p.m., footsteps began circling the camp.

Slow.Measured.Heavy.

Too controlled for a deer.Too soft for a moose.

Pacing.

It formed a deliberate arc around them, moving just beyond the reach of the firelight. Every time either of them shifted or stood, the footsteps paused.

When they sat still again, the pacing resumed — same rhythm, same speed, same distance.

Not stalking. Not fleeing.

Patterning.

7. The Whistle They Already Knew

At 10:47 p.m., a whistle cut through the trees.

Two rising notes. Clear. Sharp. Deliberate.

The exact whistle captured faintly in the 2009 audio — the same cadence the couple described moments before seeing the figure behind their cabin.

A second whistle answered from further in the forest. Then a third, deeper still.

A formation. A triangle.

"Three units," Jensen wrote in his notes. "Communication pattern."

The pacing did not stop.

8. Stones in the Dark

At 11:13, a small stone landed near Jensen's boot.

Then another struck one of their metal mugs with a clean, ringing **ping**.

Then silence.

Mark later told me:

"It wanted us to know it was there, but not how close."

The pacing continued.Narrower now.

Always outside the firelight, but always present.

9. The Mimicry

Shortly before midnight, the mimicry began.

First Mark's name.Calm voice.Measured cadence.Wrong rhythm.

Then Jensen's name.

Then Mark's again — slightly better mimicked the second time.

They didn't answer.They didn't move.They didn't shine lights.

Mimicry is a test.A lure.A measuring tool.

You don't engage with it.

You wait.

10. The Trees Fall

At 12:09 a.m., a tree came down behind the unseen cabin.

Fresh fall.Clean break.No wind.

Two minutes later, another fell to their right.

A third fell behind them.

Not random.Not natural.

A boundary.

A triangle around their camp.

11. The Cabin Door Opens

They could not see the cabin from where they camped.But at 12:23 a.m., they heard its door open.

A long, dragging creak as the swollen frame gave way under a force that should not have been able to move it.

Mark wrote:

"It sounded like someone opening a throat.Wet wood. Slow pressure. Nothing natural."

The door finished its arc and settled.

Then nothing.

Nothing except the sensation of being noticed.

12. The Final Circle and the Exhale

At 1:02 a.m., the footsteps began circling tighter.

Closer.Heavier.Deliberate.

Then—

A single, massive exhale sounded behind their camp.

Chest-deep. Wet. Animal — but not like any animal they knew.

That was the breaking point.

They didn't run. Professionals don't run in Temagami at night.

They quietly packed the essentials, snuffed the fire, and moved out along the same path they came in, headlamps dimmed low.

The pacing did not follow. The forest remained silent.

But they felt watched until they reached the shoreline.

13. The Island Refuge

They pushed off in the canoe and paddled toward a small island they had passed earlier.

Open water felt safer. The air felt different — lighter, less compressed.

On the island, they set up a minimal camp and kept a small fire going more for morale than light.

No footsteps. No whistles. No stones. No mimicry.

For the first time all night, the woods felt normal again.

They slept in fragments, but they slept.

By dawn, the ridge felt like another world — one they had crossed into and barely crossed back out of.

When they paddled out the next morning, neither of them looked toward the cabin's ridge.

Sometimes not seeing is its own kind of mercy

Chapter 19 — STRANGE LIGHTS OVER BLACKWATER LAKES

Silent Orbs, Aerial Gliders, and the Intelligent Lights Witnesses See Moving Above Temagami's Deepest Waters

1. The Sky Has Its Own Set of Watchers

Temagami is known for its water.Its forests.Its ridges.Its ancient rock.

But above all that — literally — is another layer of the mystery.

On quiet nights, when the lake becomes a perfect mirror and the wind drops to nothing, witnesses describe lights drifting across the sky:

- silent
- purposeful
- gliding
- sometimes fast, sometimes impossibly slow
- often hovering directly above deep water

These aren't satellites.Aren't aircraft.Aren't drones.

They move the wrong way.Change direction too sharply.Dim and brighten with intention.

People describe them as:

"the watchers of the sky."

And what's disturbing is how often they appear directly over the deepest blackwater lakes — the same lakes associated with underwater creatures, vanishings, missing time, and strange vibrations from beneath.

Some locals believe:

"The sky lights and the lake shadows are connected."

After hearing these stories, I believe they might be right.

2. The Silent Light Over Temagami Lake

One of the earliest modern accounts came from a couple stargazing on a warm July night along Temagami's southern shore.

They sat on a flat rock shelf watching the Milky Way rise over the treeline.

Then a single white orb appeared above the lake —not falling, not shooting, not blinking.

Just **there.**

It drifted sideways — horizontally — at a slow, smooth pace, maintaining perfect altitude.

No sound. No trail. No flicker.

The woman said:

"It was like someone moving a flashlight behind a curtain."

The orb hovered directly above the deepest part of the lake for nearly twenty seconds, then shot upward so fast it disappeared instantly — leaving no trace.

Not a meteor.Not a plane.Not anything familiar.

The man said:

"My brain doesn't even know what category to put that in."

3. The Fishermen Who Saw Three Lights Move in Triangle Formation

Three night anglers on Sharp Rock Inlet spotted three lights in the sky arranged in a perfect triangle.

They assumed they were aircraft.

But then the lights began to move:

- rising
- falling
- shifting sideways
- circling one another
- forming and reforming geometric patterns

The lights moved like **a single unit with multiple points**, weaving above the treeline in ways no aircraft can.

One fisherman said:

"It wasn't three objects.

It was one thing with three lights."

The triangle drifted toward the center of the lake —paused —then collapsed inward, merging into a single bright orb before streaking across the sky in a sharp, angled path.

Aircraft don't merge. Drones don't form spirals. Satellites don't zigzag.

But these lights did.

4. The Orb That Followed a Canoe

Two paddlers returning from a late evening excursion on Ferguson Bay saw a pale light appear above the treeline.

They watched it drift toward them, low and steady.

It hovered above the water, about eighty feet overhead, following their canoe's path for several minutes.

They tried paddling faster. The orb adjusted.

Slower. The orb adjusted.

When they turned toward shore, the orb followed.

The younger paddler whispered:

"It's tracking us."

Just before they reached land, the orb ascended quickly straight upward and vanished.

The older paddler said:

"I wasn't scared until it matched our speed.

That's when I knew it wasn't something natural."

5. The Red Light That Rose From the Lake Itself

A man camping near the deep waters of Kokoko saw a dull red glow beneath the lake surface at midnight.

At first, he thought it was his eyes adjusting to the dark.

But the glow brightened.

It rose from beneath the water —slowly —until it broke the surface.

A perfect sphere of red light hovered three feet above the lake.

No dripping water. No steam. Just hovering.

After several seconds, it drifted upward, rising silently to treetop height before shooting horizontally across the lake and vanishing.

He said:

"I know what I saw.

It came out of the water."

This account aligns with several others from deeper Temagami lakes.

6. The Floating Light Seen by Five Canoes on Diamond Lake

In one of the most credible multi-witness events, five canoes returning from an evening paddle saw a light hovering just above the lake surface.

The light:

- glowed white-blue
- hovered about six feet above the water
- moved slowly across the lake
- reflected gently, without distortion
- made no sound

The group paddled closer — cautiously.

The light began to rise, smoothly, vertically, as if lifting by invisible strings.

At a height of about fifty feet, it stopped.

Hovered.

Then dimmed until it was nothing more than a faint pinprick — and winked out.

One paddler said:

"It was observing us.

I swear it waited until we got close before it left."

7. The Light That Traveled Below the Treetops

A pair of local guides traveling by boat late one autumn night saw a glowing orb weaving through the treeline — not above it. Through it.

They could see the light passing between trunks, illuminating branches as it moved.

The orb descended toward the lake, then rose again, passed through a stand of tall pines, and disappeared behind a ridgeline.

The guides know aircraft. They know drones. They know flares.

This wasn't any of those.

One guide said:

"Whatever it was, it had control.

Perfect control."

8. Why These Lights Aren't Satellites, Aircraft, or Drones

Skeptics often default to the usual explanations:

- drones

- satellites
- aircraft
- planets
- fireworks
- reflections

But each explanation fails for at least one reason —and often several:

- Satellites don't stop, hover, or change direction.

-Aircraft need sound and navigational lights.

- Drones cannot travel the distances or durations reported.

- Flares drift randomly and extinguish quickly.

- Planets do not zigzag or descend behind trees.

- Reflections don't track canoe speed.

Witnesses aren't inexperienced observers.Many are:

- pilots
- guides
- hunters
- fire rangers

- seasoned canoeists

People who know the sky.People who know the lake.People who know what's normal.

These lights are not normal.

9. The Connection Between Lights and Water

One detail recurs in nearly every account:

The lights appear most frequently above the deepest water.

Not above campsites.Not over ridges.Not along trails.

Always:

- deep pockets
- trenches
- cold blackwater basins
- underwater cliffs
- ancient lakebeds

These same areas coincide with:

- lake creature sightings
- missing canoeists
- strange sounds from below

- time distortion events
- cloaked presences
- hominid sightings
- ridge walkers

It's as if Temagami has **vertical layers** of mystery:

- the sky
- the surface
- the forest
- the depths

And something moves between them.

One witness said:

"The lights above the lake felt connected to what was in the lake."

That idea, once you hear it, becomes hard to shake.

10. What the Strange Lights Reveal About the Larger Mystery

This chapter isn't about aliens or ships.This isn't science fiction.

These lights behave like:

- sensors

- scouts
- signals
- or environmental anomalies tied to deeper forces

Their patterns match those of the watchers, silent ones, and lake creatures:

- deliberate
- observant
- evasive
- intelligent

If the lake creatures are the oldest beings of the water, and the watchers rule the forest, the lights may be the **third domain**:

The watchers of the sky.

Their presence deepens the central idea of this book:

Temagami is not empty wilderness. Temagami is layered. Populated. Observed. And far older than we understand.

CHAPTER 20 — HAUNTED CAMPSITES OF OLD GROWTH TEMAGAMI

Phantom Footsteps, Vanishing Camps, Cooking Sounds on Empty Islands, and the Residual Work of Long-Gone Men

1. The Places Campers Don't Talk About Afterward

Some regions of Temagami feel strange after dark — not because of animals, not because of the wind, but because of something else.

A kind of awareness.

An old pressure.

Certain campsites, especially those near age-old logging routes, trapping cabins, and small cedar-wrapped islands, have a reputation that spreads quietly among paddlers:

"Don't camp there if you want to sleep."

Not because you'll be attacked — but because the forest remembers.

And sometimes, the forest repeats.

2. The Island Cabin That Sounds Alive at Night

One of the most documented hauntings in your archival notes involves a small island cabin — abandoned, collapsing, and yet somehow still "occupied" long after dark.

A couple who camped across from the island in 2019 described three nights that changed their view of Temagami forever.

Night One — Cooking Sounds

They heard:

- chopping
- footsteps
- pots rattling
- water pouring
- something heavy dragged across a floor
- low humming

All coming from the cabin.Which is empty.Has been for decades.No dishes, no tools, no living space.

Yet the soundscape resembled a man preparing a late meal.

Every detail is preserved in your file, including their direct description:

"It sounded like someone cooking for a logging crew."

Night Two — Male Voices

The next night brought knocking from across the water…followed by a door slam…then the unmistakable sound of conversation.

Your notes capture it perfectly:

"Mellow… conversational… almost like men around a fire."

Not angry voices.Not shouting.

Work voices.End-of-day voices.

Night Three — Silence

The cabin fell silent.

Not calm silent.Dead silent.

The couple said the stillness felt "held," as if someone — or something — was waiting.

When they paddled over in the morning, they found:

- a chair shifted
- a muddy footprint in the corner
- a tin cup on the floor

No other sign of occupancy.

The footprint was the only physical trace.

They left Temagami the same afternoon.

3. The Feeling of Being Watched — But Not From the Treeline

A recurring line in your document stood out immediately:

"Almost everyone feels watched —not from the woods…but from inside the cabin."

This is unusual.

Most wilderness hauntings involve:

- shapes in the trees
- shadows near camp
- footsteps around tents

But this one centers on an interior.

An empty cabin.

Witnesses consistently describe:

- hairs rising on arms
- pressure on chest
- a presence in the corner
- a figure behind the window

Some even report hearing a soft shuffle inside when they turn away.

One group sprinted back to their canoe after hearing a single footstep —just one —from the cabin's dark interior.

4. The Paddle-By That Went Wrong (2022)

One of the most chilling encounters in your file happened when three paddlers approached the island after hearing the usual chopping and cooking noises.

As they neared the shore, the cabin door opened.

Slowly. On its own.

Your notes record it exactly:

"The door stayed open."

Then came:

- a single step on the wooden floor
- slow, deep breathing **from inside**

The paddlers turned their canoe around without looking back.

This detail aligns precisely with residual hauntings —patterns that replay but occasionally **acknowledge** the living.

5. Campsite Resets — When the Forest Rearranges Your Gear

Some of the most disturbing stories in your file are not violent or dramatic.

They are subtle.

Almost polite.

The Campsite That Rebuilt Itself

A storm knocked down a tarp, scattered a firepit, and rolled a log four feet away.

By morning everything was:

- rebuilt
- replaced
- re-knotted
- reorganized

Exactly as before.

Even a twig used to prop a knife was put back.

As your notes say:

"Everything was exact."

No animal could do that.

No person could do it silently.

The Campsite That Was Completely Erased

Another paddler woke to find her entire campsite **gone** — firepit, woodpile, bootprints, even tent impressions.

Only the tent remained.

The ground looked untouched, as if she had never camped there.

Your file records her reaction:

"I felt unwelcome… like the forest wanted solitude."

This is not mischief.

This is **erasure**.

A boundary marker.

The Campsite That Was Moved 70 Meters

Two hunters returned to find their entire setup — tents, chairs, coolers — moved neatly to another clearing **with no tracks** and no signs of dragging.

Your notes emphasize the impossibility:

"No drag marks. No signs of struggle."

This suggests:

- unseen presence
- organization
- intent
- a need for order

- or territorial behavior

Your file further concludes:

"Something corrects or erases evidence of human presence."

6. The Invisible Wagon — Ghost Sounds on Old Logging Roads

One of the most cinematic stories in your file is the Invisible Wagon haunting near Anima Nipissing:

Witnesses heard:

- horses snorting
- wooden wheels creaking
- chains
- rhythmic hoof steps

It passed within **ten feet** of their tent — with sound, pressure, and vibration — yet absolutely no visible wagon, no animals, no cargo.

One camper cried afterward from the emotional weight of the moment.

This detail comes directly from your file:

"It felt like men working… but they weren't here. Not anymore."

Residual haunting at its purest.

Temagami remembers its past.

And sometimes the past walks the old roads again.

7. The Timber Splash at Midnight

Multiple reports in your file describe a massive splash echoing through valleys — as if tons of timber were dumped into water.

But these events occur:

- on dry ridges
- far from lakes
- with no evidence of impact
- no broken trees
- no water

Your file suggests this is a ghost echo of early logging "splash dam" releases.

A sound out of time.

A memory replaying itself.

This aligns perfectly with the idea of Temagami as a **thin place** — a land layered with history so heavy it leaks into the present.

8. Why These Hauntings Don't Follow Typical Ghost Patterns

The haunting material in your file reveals several unusual consistencies:

1. They are overwhelmingly auditory. Chopping, footsteps, knocks, wagon sounds.

2. Visual apparitions are rare — but focused and purposeful.

3. Campsite manipulation is precise — not chaotic. Rebuilt campfires. Tidied objects. Complete erasure.

4. Hauntings cluster around:

- old cabins
- historic roadbeds
- logging spurs
- islands
- deep lakes
- thin-place areas

5. Events often align with historic logging rhythms: Dawn starting shifts, late-night returns.

Your file summarizes this neatly:

"Ghosts aren't hunting. They're working."

Temagami's hauntings appear to be **residual activity** — motion, sound, and presence repeating long after the people themselves are gone.

But some events — like the breathing inside the cabin or the campsite rearrangements — show awareness.

Reciprocity.

A response to the living.

9. What These Hauntings Add to the Larger Temagami Mystery

Until now this book has focused on:

- hominid watchers
- cloaked presences
- ridge walkers
- lake creatures
- sky lights

But the haunting evidence adds a new dimension:

The land remembers —and the memory is active.

These hauntings are not isolated from the physical phenomena.

They overlay it.

Share locations with it.

Occur on the same nights as:

- mimicry
- pacing

- vanishing camps
- deep lake hums
- cloaked movements

If the watchers are beings of the forest, the hauntings may be the forest's **memory system** —echoes of labor, routine, movement, and presence layered into the land itself.

CHAPTER 21 — THE WOMAN ON THE WATER

Lake Apparitions, Fog-Shrouded Figures, Paddle Echoes in Empty Bays, and the Ghost Stories Temagami Locals Avoid Telling Out Loud

1. The Oldest Ghost Stories Are on the Water

For all the hominid sightings and unknown creatures in Temagami, the oldest stories — the ones whispered by guides, shared between paddlers at dusk, and carefully avoided by outfitters — belong to the lakes.

Not the ridges. Not the forests.

The water.

In Temagami, the deepest lakes feel ancient in a different way. People report strange lights above them, massive creatures below them, and something else entirely drifting *on* them:

Figures on the water that shouldn't exist.

Most commonly:

- a woman in white or grey, gliding through fog
- a canoe-shaped shadow with no paddler
- a silhouette pacing atop the waterline

- voices carrying across the lake with no source
- paddling sounds echoing from empty bays
- reflections of people who are not there

The hauntings here don't behave like the cabin or campsite phenomena.

They are quieter.More distant.More grief-like.

And the presence most often described is the same:

The Woman on the Water.

2. The Fog-Ghost of Lady Evelyn Lake

Lady Evelyn has some of the darkest water in Temagami.Deep.Still.Darker than ink on moonless nights.

Decades of paddlers have reported sightings on that lake, but one story stands out — the one nearly identical across multiple witnesses, years apart.

A pair of paddlers drifting through early morning fog heard a faint splash behind them.

They turned.

In the fog hovered a shape.A tall, thin outline of a woman —almost luminous,but not bright,as if cut out of the mist itself.

She glided slowly across the water,not quite above it,not quite on it —somewhere between reflection and form.

Her head was down.Her arms hung loosely at her sides.The hem of her shape trailed like fabric in current.

The paddlers remained motionless, whispering:

"Do you see her too?"

When one of them called out,the figure stopped.

Not faded —stopped.Paused.

Then she drifted backward into the fog and dissolved.

Both paddlers agreed on the same unsettling detail:

There was **no ripple** on the water.

3. The Canoe With No Paddler

One of the most unsettling water hauntings involves the sound of paddling echoing across lakes with no visible canoe.

A guide and client fishing near Sharp Rock Inlet heard canoe strokes in the stillness.

Not random splashes.Long, slow, deliberate paddling.The rhythm of someone traveling at a steady pace.

The sound grew closer.

They scanned the lake.

No canoe.No kayak.No wind.No waves.

But the sound kept coming —moving past their boat,then into an adjacent bay,then fading into the distance.

The guide whispered:

"That was a canoe.

There was just no canoe."

This fits the broader pattern:

Residual travel hauntings —echoes of old canoe routes still replaying across blackwater.

4. The Reflection That Wasn't Anyone's

One of the strangest lake hauntings comes from a paddler who set up a camera to take a long-exposure shot of his canoe beached on shore.

The lake was perfectly still.

In the image he captured afterward:

- his canoe
- the shoreline
- the trees behind him

And a faint, translucent figure standing knee-deep in the water beside his canoe.

A woman.

Tall.Hair draped downward.Face indistinct.

He hadn't seen her.He hadn't heard her.She didn't appear in the moment —only in the reflection captured by the lens.

This mirrors the "Blue Visitor" phenomenon in your file, which also appeared only in long-exposure as a tall luminous blur.

Some entities in Temagami appear more easily in reflection than in direct sight — as if mirrors, water, and long exposures provide a different access point to the world they occupy.

5. The Woman Seen Kneeling on the Ice

Temagami winters are long and brutal.But the hauntings don't stop just because the lakes freeze.

A trapper crossing Red Squirrel Lake in mid-winter saw a woman kneeling on the ice roughly 200 meters ahead.

She was still.Head bowed.Hands on the surface.

He shouted.

She didn't move.

He approached slowly, feeling a tightness in his chest.

When he was within fifty meters, he realized:

She had no shadow.

He blinked — and she vanished.

Left behind was a small patch of frost shaped like the impression of two hands.

This detail echoes another winter haunting:**The Snow Walkers**, briefly mentioned in your original draft as tall, silent figures crossing frozen lakes.

6. The Voice From the Middle of the Lake

Several paddlers have described hearing:

- a woman calling
- a woman humming
- or a woman crying softly

from the center of a lake.

Not the shore.Not nearby camps.

The center.

One account describes a woman's voice echoing on Diamond Lake during a dead-calmed night.

The paddlers woke to soft crying drifting from the water —not ghost-wail crying,but something human,sad,restrained.

When they paddled toward the sound,it moved away —slowly, deliberately —as if leading them.

They stopped paddling.The crying stopped.

The moment they pushed forward again,it resumed.

They turned back.

The crying returned immediately behind them.

After an hour of confusion and fear,they paddled to shore and built a fire.

One said:

"It wasn't trying to scare us.

It wanted us to follow."

7. The Woman on the Water — Who Is She?

Several theories for Temagami apparitions:

- a lone trapper
- a logging cook
- a prospector
- residual work memories
- a "thin place" echo
- something older than humanity
- a figure seen between worlds

Those apply to land hauntings — but the water presence is different.

Witness descriptions suggest:

- she appears only in low light
- only on calm water
- only near deep basins

- never approaches camps
- never threatens
- always moves slowly
- often drifts *backwards*, not forward
- appears in fog more than clear nights

Locals often give the same explanation:

"She drowned."

"She's looking for someone."

"She's trapped in the fog."

"She's rowing a route she never finished."

But these are just attempts to make sense of something much older.

Because the earliest Indigenous stories in the region — the ones rarely written down — mention a woman-spirit associated with:

- cold water
- deep places
- fog
- transitions
- boundaries
- grief
- and the "thin veil" between worlds

Not malevolent. Not hostile.

A traveler between places.

A messenger.

8. Eyewitness Patterns Across the File

When I compare all lake-haunting accounts — both from your original file and outside reports — the patterns align:

1. She is not a threat.

She never approaches. Never touches. Never interacts directly.

2. She is residual.

She appears like a recording — but one that reacts slightly to attention.

3. She is bound to water.

Never land-based. Never on shore.

4. She is most active:

- in fog
- at dawn
- at dusk
- during absolute calm

- over extremely deep water

5. Her presence often coincides with other phenomena:

- floating orbs
- underwater hums
- unknown swimmers
- time distortion
- missing canoes

All of which were documented earlier in this book.

The haunting is not separate from the larger Temagami mystery.

It is another layer of it.

The **sky watchers**, the **ridge walkers**, the **lake creatures**, the **night visitors**, the **invisible wagon**, the **cabin cook**, and now **the woman on the water** all align into one principle:

Temagami is not singularly haunted. It is multiply haunted — by memory, by presence, and by beings that do not act like ghosts at all.

9. What the Water Hauntings Mean

Hauntings on water are different from land hauntings everywhere in the world.

They are:

- more solemn
- more residual
- more tragic

But in Temagami, they also appear **connected** to:

- the underwater creatures
- the strange lights
- the deep-lake hum
- missing time
- vanishings
- cloaked presences at shorelines

It's as if the water is another threshold —a place where whatever occupies Temagami's darker layers rises closest to the surface.

The woman on the water may not be a ghost.

She may be:

- a memory
- an echo
- a boundary guardian
- a remnant of something older

Or, like the Blue Visitor in your file, a figure from "between worlds," seen only when the conditions are right.

Whatever she is, she is part of the pattern.

CHAPTER 22 — PREDATORS THAT AREN'T BEARS
Shadow Wolves, Silent Pursuers, and the Tall, Dark Shapes That Stalk Camps But Leave No Tracks

1. When Something Follows You and You Know It's Not a Bear

In Temagami, there are animals that follow you through the woods.

Bears do it. Wolves do it. Moose sometimes do it out of pure stubborn curiosity.

But what people describe in these encounters doesn't match any known predator. Not by movement. Not by sound. Not by pacing. Not by silhouette.

Witnesses report:

- footsteps that are too heavy for wolves
- breathing too deep for any canine
- shapes too tall for bears
- movement too precise for moose
- eyeshine too high to be natural
- stalking behavior too intelligent to be wildlife

And strangest of all:

They follow without breaking brush.

You can't walk ten steps through Temagami forest without snapping something —yet these things move silently, matching your pace, staying just beyond the treeline.

When people say, *"Something followed us last night,"* they don't mean an animal.

They mean something else.

2. The Heavy Footsteps on the Ridge

One pair of campers near Sharp Rock Inlet reported something pacing them from the moment they left camp for a night paddle.

The footsteps:

- paralleled their canoe from the ridge
- kept perfect pace
- were heavy enough to thud through the granite layer
- never paused, never stumbled
- never broke a branch

When they stopped paddling, the steps stopped.

When they continued, the steps resumed.

A bear? Impossible — bears crash. They grunt. They huff. They break twigs with every third step.

This thing moved:

- rhythmically
- deliberately
- intelligently

Once, it shifted downslope to keep them in line of sight. That maneuver alone eliminated any natural animal.

One of the paddlers whispered later:

"It was walking on two feet.

I don't care what anyone says.

That was upright movement."

3. The Shadow That Tracked a Family For Three Nights

This account comes from the northern edge of Temagami, close to one of the least-traveled lakes — an area that, in your original notes, already had sightings of cloaked presences and moving silhouettes.

A family camping on a peninsula noticed something odd on the first night:

A tall, dark outline lingering near the trees at dusk.

The father dismissed it as a burned snag. But later, he looked again — and the shape was gone.

The second night, they heard:

- slow steps
- deliberate breathing
- a low rumble
- shifting weight behind the tent

The father called out with a loud "HEY!" and the thing stepped back.

Not ran back. Stepped. One heavy, controlled movement.

On the third night, the shape returned — standing at the edge of the treeline, swaying slightly, as if trying to see around the firelight.

Not a bear. Not a moose. Not anything of this world that walks on four legs.

The mother said:

"It watched from behind a pine.

Tall.

Too tall."

After several minutes, it simply backed away into the dark.

No sound.

Nothing natural moves like that.

4. The Wolf Pack That Refused to Enter an Area

This story was brought up by a Temagami guide who has spent over twenty-five years in the backcountry.

He watched a wolf pack travel along a pressure ridge of snow late one winter evening. They were confident, moving in formation, until they reached a certain clearing.

Then they stopped.

All of them.

No growling. No snarling. No interest in crossing at all.

The alpha stood perfectly still, staring into the trees.

Then — without a sound — the pack changed direction, circled wide, and avoided the clearing entirely.

Wolves are bold animals. They don't abort routes for no reason.

When the guide walked the area the next morning, he found:

- large impressions in the snow
- long strides
- deep heel pressure
- a bipedal gait
- something at least 8 feet tall

No claw marks. No pads.

Just footprints shaped like a human's — but far too big, and spaced far too long.

He said:

"Whatever it was,

the wolves wanted no part of it."

5. The Silent Stalker on the Old Portage Route

Near the Obabika Triangle, two friends traveling a forgotten portage heard something pacing behind them.

It wasn't breaking brush.

It wasn't breathing loudly.

It wasn't trying to hide.

It simply matched their walking rhythm:

- step
- step
- step

always a few paces behind, always stopping exactly when they did.

The pair pretended not to notice, but one of them later said:

"It was studying us."

"Not hunting.

Studying."

When they reached the lake, the footsteps vanished —not faded,not diminished.

Just vanished.

No creature leaves without making a sound at the moment of departure…unless it stepped off the trail into someplace quieter than the forest floor.

Or unless it was never fully within our world to begin with.

6. Night Growls That Don't Belong to Any Known Species

Several campers across multiple lakes describe hearing deep, resonant growls at night —too low for wolves,too bass-heavy for bears,too guttural for cougars (rare here anyway).

These growls vibrate through the tent floor.They come from just outside the firelight.They rumble with a density that feels wrong.

One hunter said:

"It sounded like a bear the size of a car.

But heavier.

More chest behind it."

What frightens these witnesses most isn't the sound…it's the silence afterward.

Animals shuffle, breathe, snort, exhale.

These beings don't.

They growl —once —then go silent.

Total silent.

Predators never act like that.

But watchers do.

7. The Tall Thing at the Tree Line

One of the eeriest patterns emerges from repeated witness descriptions:

A tall, thin, dark shape standing between the trees.

Not crouched like a bear.Not hunched like a moose.Not broad like a wolf.

Tall.Straight.Still.

Often 8 to 9 feet high.Sometimes more.

The shape appears at:

- dusk
- midnight
- early dawn

And disappears not by turning away,but by simply not being there anymore.

Some describe the disappearance as a "blink" —like an abrupt visual glitch in the treeline.

This links directly to your earlier chapters on cloaked beings and the ridge walkers.

Sometimes people see the watchers.Sometimes they only see their silhouette.

Either way, the effect is the same:

The feeling of being observed by something that towers above any known forest predator.

8. Predator Behavior Without Predator Biology

The most disturbing detail across all these accounts is consistency in **behavior**:

These beings:

- track silently
- flank intelligently
- stay downwind
- maintain distance
- avoid firelight
- keep to blind spots
- use the terrain strategically
- circle camps without entering

- retreat when confronted
- return later that night

This is **predatory intelligence** without **predatory intent**.

As though you are being monitored, not hunted.

Studied, not stalked.

Measured, not taken.

This aligns with earlier land-based sightings: the pacing at cabins, the watchers near canoes, the forest rearranging itself, and the "presence" described in your haunting file.

Something is patrolling Temagami.

Something territorial.

Something that knows how to move without making a sound.

9. What These Encounters Suggest About the Larger Unknown

The beings described in this chapter are not:

- bears
- wolves
- moose
- wolverines

- humans
- or anything documented in Northern Ontario

Their size, intelligence, silence, and presence all suggest beings that overlap with Bigfoot-type sightings — yet behave differently:

- more patient
- less physical
- more shadow-like
- more aware
- more deliberate

If the watchers described earlier are the dominant forest intelligence, these predators-that-aren't-bears appear to be **their enforcers**, or perhaps another branch entirely.

Their behavior mirrors the deeper mystery of Temagami:

The forest is not empty. The forest is aware. And the forest is not always physical.

These encounters also align with the upcoming themes — because the next chapter takes us into the darkest part of Temagami's wilderness:

The places where sound changes, where screams are not always animal, and where people feel something ancient just behind them.

CHAPTER 23 — THE SCREAMING FOREST

Unnatural Cries, Voices That Rise From Nowhere, and the Night When the Woods Themselves Seem to Call Out

1. The Night Sounds No One Wants to Hear Twice

Every wilderness has its noises.

Owls.Coyotes.Wind in the branches.The sudden snap of a twig that jolts you awake.

Temagami has those too.But there are other sounds — sounds that do not belong to any known creature,sounds that shake people on a level deeper than fear.

Witnesses describe:

- high-pitched screams not made by any natural animal
- deep roars that fade into human-like moans
- voices that call out names no one in camp recognizes
- children crying where there are no children
- metallic groans through the trees
- long, drawn-out "wailing" rising from ravines

- layered screams, as if multiple voices are stacked on one another
- echoes of something large crashing, though no tree ever falls

These sounds don't move through the forest like hunting animals or lost hikers or wounded wildlife.

They seem to **emanate from the forest itself**.

As though the land is speaking.

Calling.

Or warning.

2. The First Scream — Sharp, Too Human, Too Close

One of the most credible accounts comes from a trio of experienced paddlers who set camp near a narrow peninsula on Lake Temagami.

They were talking quietly around the fire when it happened.

A scream —sharp, shrill, holding too much air for any human lungs, and too much pain for anything natural.

It came from directly behind their tents.

Not from afar. Not across the water.

Just behind them.

They described it the same way:

"It sounded like a woman screaming…but bigger…deeper…wrong."

The scream echoed across the lake and seemed to fold back on itself, like a sound bouncing off invisible walls.

They froze.

No one moved. No one breathed. No one spoke.

The scream came again —this time farther away, moving too quickly for any animal to create that much distance.

Within seconds, it sounded like it was across the lake.

Then higher up the ridge.

Then gone.

They never returned to that campsite.

3. The Deep Roar That Turned Into a Cry

Near Diamond Lake, a group camping along a slope heard a deep roar— something like a bear —except it rose into a pitch far beyond a bear's range.

The roar warped into something almost human.

They said:

"It sounded like a man crying…but pushed through an animal's throat."

The roar-cry repeated three times, each time moving in the wrong direction —zigzagging across the landscape in a pattern impossible for wildlife.

One camper vomited from fear. Another curled into a ball in his sleeping bag and cried.

They all felt the same after:

"We shouldn't have heard that.

We were never supposed to hear that."

4. The Wailing From the Ravine

In a steep ravine near Obabika, two canoeists portaging late in the evening heard a series of cries rising from below.

Not screams. Not animal calls.

Wailing.

Long, drawn-out, trembling sound— a sound soaked with despair —rising from the forest floor.

When they stopped, the wailing stopped.

When they took another step, the wailing resumed —closer.

One man whispered:

"It's following us."

But wailing doesn't follow. Crying doesn't track people. And the sound was not directional —it was everywhere and nowhere.

Later they said it felt like the forest was grieving.

The ravine was quiet the next morning.

5. Voices That Call Out Names — Names No One Recognizes

Several groups have reported voices calling out at night.

But not random voices.

Voices **calling names**.

Not their names.Not names they recognize.Names that feel:

- old
- heavy
- not local
- spoken in a breathy, almost ancient way

One father camping with his teenage sons described hearing:

"Maa… reeah…"

Not a name they knew.Not shouted.Just breathed through the forest.

The next night came another voice:

"Hael… ruun…"

Soft.Gentle.Almost whispered through layers of trees.

Voices that stop when you listen too closely. Voices that resume when you turn away.

Voices no one forgets.

6. The Metallic Scream on the Old Roadbed

Along an abandoned logging road near Maple Mountain, two hikers heard a scream that sounded like metal being bent in half.

A long, wrenching screech —like steel under impossible pressure —echoed through the trees.

They both instinctively covered their ears.

It went on for ten seconds, dipped into a lower tone, then let out a sharp metallic pang…then silence.

The oddest part?

There was no echo.

No forest reverberation.

It was as if the sound existed only within a bubble around them.

One hiker said:

"It sounded industrial…

but it felt alive."

There are no mines active in that region. No heavy machinery. No reason for metal to scream.

Unless it wasn't metal.

7. The Layered Scream — Multiple Voices in One

Near Anima Nipissing, a couple reported hearing what they described as "one scream containing five screams."

A single voice— but stacked, layered —like multiple beings crying out through one throat.

The sound rose through the trees, grew louder, then cut off instantly.

Layered screams appear rarely in wilderness haunting accounts. They are almost always associated with:

- thin places
- traumatic events
- or non-human entities mimicking humans in a way humans cannot fully understand

The couple left the site at first light.

They said their deepest fear wasn't the volume or the pitch, but the unnatural layering:

"Nothing living has five voices."

8. Screams That Travel Wrong

One of the strangest patterns in these accounts is how the sounds **move**.

Animals run. They change direction naturally. They break branches. They shift volume gradually as they move.

But these screams:

- jump from place to place
- leap across the landscape
- appear behind you then in front within seconds
- grow louder without approaching
- move without brushing a single branch
- cease instantly

This suggests two unsettling possibilities:

1. The source moves impossibly fast

or

2. The sound is not travel-based — it manifests

Like a broadcast. Like an echo of something long gone. Or like a mimicry performed by the unknown beings that already stalk Temagami's deeper forests.

Either way, the effect is the same:

You feel hunted by sound.

Not by a creature. By sound itself.

9. What the Screaming Forest Reveals

The screams and cries of Temagami are not random wilderness noise.

They follow patterns:

- appear near deep ravines
- cluster around old-growth areas
- coincide with mimicry events
- occur more often on moonless nights
- align with sightings of ridge walkers
- often precede predators-that-aren't-bears
- spike during periods of unusual lake activity

It's all connected.

The forest watchers.The underwater beings.The ghostly apparitions.The cloaked presences.The campsite manipulations.The sky lights.

Even the screaming forest.

Each chapter you've approved has built a single idea:

Temagami is alive.Alive in ways we do not understand.Alive in ways that contradict biology, physics, and folklore.

The screaming forest may be:

- communication

- warning

- territorial assertion

- mimicry

- or something older— something expressing itself through soundbecause we cannot see what is making it.

But the next chapter takes us somewhere even darker:

Not sounds.

Not screams.

Not echoes.

But places in Temagami where the land feels like it has been abandoned by light, hope, and human presence entirely.

Places even the watchers avoid.

CHAPTER 24 — THE DESOLATE PLACES

Dead Zones, Silent Valleys, Lost Trails, and the Parts of Temagami Where Even the Animals Refuse to Stay

1. The Wilderness Has Places That Feel Wrong

There are parts of Temagami that feel wild, untamed, ancient — but still welcoming.

Then there are other places.

Places that don't want you there.

Places that feel hollow.Empty.Drained.

These are the **Desolate Places** — a scattered network of small valleys, ridges, bogs, and island interiors where something is deeply, fundamentally off.

Witnesses describe:

- silence so complete their heartbeat feels too loud
- trails that lead nowhere and appear to shift
- the air feeling thicker, heavier
- nausea or dizziness on entering
- animals fleeing the area entirely

- sudden dread with no visible threat
- gear malfunctioning
- voices fading out on radios
- compasses spiraling
- campfires burning strangely low
- a feeling of being watched from below, not above

These aren't just eerie spots.

They are **zones of absence**.

It's not what you hear —it's what you *don't*.

Temagami is loud. Even at night you get the crack of twigs, the flap of wings, the splash of a fish, the wind humming through old pines.

But these places?

Silent.

Still.

Desolate.

2. The Bog Where No Birds Land

One such area sits near a shallow bog north of Obabika — a place several experienced guides refuse to camp near.

The bog looks normal: green moss mats, shallow water, sunlit patches of reeds.

But no birds ever land there.

Not a single songbird,not a crow,not even the hardy little jays that normally follow canoes for crumbs.

One guide described paddling past it:

"The forest was loud on both sides.

The bog itself was like a mute button had been pressed."

Another witness walked close enough to throw a stick into it.The stick didn't splash.It landed silently —as if the water had thickened beneath it.

Later, he said:

"The silence wasn't peaceful.

It was defensive."

3. The Clearing With No Sound and No Reason

Along the Red Squirrel extension, there's a clearing that looks like a perfect place to camp:

Flat ground.Soft moss.Good tree cover.

But no one stays there twice.

A pair of hikers stopped for lunch and immediately felt lightheaded.The wind died.The insects vanished.Their voices sounded strange —slightly muffled,like they were speaking inside a room lined with cotton.

One man said:

"I heard my own voice echo back to me.

Outdoors doesn't echo."

They left after ten minutes and felt normal again as soon as they stepped out of the clearing.

Back at the outfitter, they mentioned the place casually.

The outfitter paled slightly and said:

"We don't send people there."

He had no explanation.

Just that line.

4. The Island Where Fire Won't Burn Right

One island in central Temagami has a small clearing that seems perfect for camping — except that fire behaves strangely there.

Multiple campers have reported:

- fires burning low even with dry wood
- flames tinted blue around the edges
- sparks falling straight down instead of drifting
- smoke moving upward in a tight column, unnaturally straight

One group even attempted to cook a meal, but the fire never produced enough heat to boil water.

When they moved their stove fifteen meters away, it worked perfectly.

One of them said:

"It felt like something beneath the ground was pulling the heat downward."

Another joked nervously:

"It's like the earth is hungry."

None of them slept well that night.

They left before sunrise.

5. The Valley That Eats Sound

Near the Temagami River, there is a long, narrow valley known among certain guides as *the place where sound goes to die.*

Voices don't travel in that valley.

Shouts come out weak and short. Footsteps seem to sink into the moss without echo. Tree snaps sound distant.

Three hikers attempted to call from opposite ends of the valley.

They couldn't hear each other at all.

One hiker described the feeling perfectly:

"It felt like someone had turned the world down.

Like I was walking through someone else's dream."

And they all reported the same thing:

A constant pressure in the chest — not pain, just weight.

As if the valley was sitting on their ribs.

6. The Animals Won't Enter These Places

Every witness who brings dogs, pack animals, or encounters wildlife notices the same thing:

Animals stop at the boundary. They refuse to enter.

Dogs whine and sit down. Moose detour around the zones. Even squirrels avoid the branches over those clearings.

One hunter described watching a wolf pack skirt a bog by nearly a kilometer — an unnecessarily wide arc.

He said:

"Wolves don't waste energy.

They give places meaning.

If they avoid it, so should you."

It's not just avoidance. It's fear.

The animals know something we don't.

7. The Portage That No Longer Leads Anywhere

One of the strangest desolate places is an old portage trail that appears on several historic maps — a thin line running between two narrow lakes.

Except it no longer exists.

Not overgrown. Not lost to storms. Not reclaimed by forest.

Just... *gone*.

A pair of experienced canoeists attempted to follow the faint outline of the portage, but after fifty meters, the trail faded into a blank patch of forest floor.

No stumps. No cut logs. No worn soil. No old blazes.

As if no one had ever walked there at all.

One of the canoeists said the experience felt like standing on a staircase that suddenly ended in midair.

"The map told us it should continue.

The forest told us it never existed."

But old trapper logs confirm it did.

Something erased the trail.

Something took it back.

8. The Feeling of Another Presence — Not Watching, But Waiting

Unlike the watchers or the predators-that-aren't-bears, these desolate places don't feel observed.

They feel **uninhabited.**

As if something left…or died…or is lying dormant beneath the earth.

People describe a sensation not of eyes on them —but of **being alone in a place that shouldn't be empty.**

The presence here is:

- hollow
- exhausted
- drained
- ancient
- indifferent
- vaguely sad

It's not curiosity. Not hostility.

It's **absence**.

And because the forest is normally alive with movement, this absence feels like a presence itself.

A void.

A void that follows you home in your memory.

9. What the Desolate Places Mean in the Larger Pattern

Across the chapters so far, Temagami has revealed layers:

- watchers in the trees
- ghostly workers in the forest
- apparitions on the water
- massive creatures deep in lakes
- lights in the sky
- predators that move without sound
- screams that travel wrong

The desolate places are different.

They are not expressions of intelligence.

They are expressions of **withdrawal**.

It's almost as if the land itself is:

- recovering from something
- hiding something
- protecting a boundary

- or holding space for something beneath the surface

And when you map the locations of these dead zones, a disturbing pattern emerges:

They form **buffers** around:

- deep lake trenches
- old-growth cedar stands
- places with recurring hominid sightings
- areas of intense sky-light activity
- historic Indigenous spiritual sites
- sudden elevation drops
- ancient water channels
- the next chapter's subject: places with abnormally large footprints and towering silhouettes

The desolate places don't exist randomly.

They form **the edges of something**.

A border.

A perimeter.

A protective ring.

Something in Temagami occupies these central areas — something the forest itself retreats from.

And in the next chapter, we step right up to that threshold:

We meet the beings that define that border.

Beings far larger than wolves, larger than bears, larger than any known forest-dwelling creature.

CHAPTER 25 — GIANTS OF TEMAGAMI

Massive Silhouettes, Tree-Breaking Footsteps, and the Colossal Beings Witnesses Describe on the Edge of the Map

1. The Footsteps That Don't Belong to Any Living Creature

There are places in Temagami — especially near the desolate zones — where people hear footsteps so heavy they feel them in their chest before they hear them in their ears.

Not stomping. Not crashing. Nothing chaotic.

Deliberate, slow, thunder-deep footsteps that seem to press the earth downward.

Witnesses report:

- ground trembling
- moss compressing several inches
- stones shaking
- echoes rolling through the understory

And most chilling of all:

These footsteps walk in straight, determined lines — not the meandering patterns of animals.

One hunter said:

"It sounded like a tree was walking."

But trees don't walk.

Something else does.

2. The Tree That Snapped at Five Feet High

Near the Sturgeon River, a guide and his two clients were exploring a section of old-growth when they came upon a tree snapped clean in half...at shoulder height.

The break was:

- fresh
- angled
- splintered outward
- not chewed
- not storm-fallen

A perfect fracture, as if something massive had gripped it and pushed until it broke.

The guide paced around the trunk in disbelief.

This wasn't a sapling —it was a fir tree as thick as a man's thigh.

He told his clients:

"A moose isn't doing that.

A bear isn't doing that.

Nothing in this forest is doing that."

One client whispered:

"Something big walked through here."

The guide didn't disagree.

He simply led them out of the area.

3. The Silhouette Across the Ravine

One of the most chilling accounts comes from two friends hiking near a high cliff overlooking a ravine.

They stopped to take a break.

Across the ravine, partially hidden behind a massive cedar, stood something tall.

Not just tall — **towering.**

They estimate the height at:

- 10 to 12 feet
- possibly more

The being wasn't hunched. Wasn't crouched. Wasn't leaning.

It was standing upright.

What they saw:

- shoulders nearly as wide as the cedar trunk
- a long arm that rested against the tree
- no visible neck
- a head that sat deep into massive shoulders
- dark, moss-colored hide or fur

But what unnerved them most was its stillness.

The being did not sway. Did not shift. Did not step.

It stood perfectly still, as if carved into the landscape.

One hiker whispered:

"It's not hiding.

It wants us to know it's there."

After almost a full minute of mutual observation, the giant turned and walked away, each step sending faint tremors through the ground beneath the hikers' boots.

4. The Paddle-By Encounter With the Giant on the Cliff

A pair of paddlers traveling at dusk on a remote lake noticed what they thought was a burnt tree trunk standing high on the cliff above them.

They paddled closer.

The trunk shifted.

Very slowly.

The "tree" straightened.

Then it stepped backward, its enormous form disappearing behind the ridge.

Both paddlers froze mid-stroke.

The giant had been:

- at least 12 feet tall
- broad enough to block out a section of sky
- perfectly upright
- staring down at them

The woman in the canoe said later:

"It watched us like we were something it had seen a thousand times.

Not prey.

Not a threat.

Just… there."

It did not approach. It did not flee.

It simply vanished behind the ridge, leaving the paddlers in a silence so deep they could hear the water settle behind their canoe.

5. The Shadow That Crossed the Road

One of the few road-based sightings happened around midnight near the gravel access route toward Temagami's north end.

A man driving alone saw something massive cross the road in front of him.

The creature was so large he first thought it was a moose.

But then he realized:

- no antlers
- no snout
- no four-legged motion
- no sloping back

The thing walked on two legs.

Long strides.Slow.Heavy.

Head swaying slightly with each step.

His headlights illuminated only the lower half —huge legs the width of tree trunks.

The upper half was too tall to be captured within his beams.He estimated the creature must have been **at least 11 feet tall**.

Once it crossed,the forest shook for several seconds with its retreating footsteps.

He kept driving until he reached town and refused to travel that road again at night.

6. The Giants Seen Standing at Water's Edge

A frightening pattern emerges in lakeside encounters:

Giant beings standing at the waterline— not moving, not drinking, not pacing, just standing.

Multiple paddlers describe:

- tall figures halfway submerged
- silhouettes with shoulders reaching above young trees
- reflections distorted and enormous
- statuesque stances, as if waiting
- long fingers hanging motionless
- heads tilted slightly toward the lake

These giants never wade in. Never pursue boats. Never vocalize.

But they are always seen in deep basins— areas where lake hums and massive underwater shadows have been recorded.

The implication is disturbing:

The giants may be connected to whatever lives in the lake beneath them. Or guarding it.

7. The Thunder-Walking Phenomenon

A recurring sign of giant presence is **thunder-walking** — a term some locals use for the heavy, slow footfalls that vibrate through the forest floor.

Witnesses describe:

- utensils rattling
- tents trembling
- fire logs shifting
- water in containers rippling
- moss pulsing underfoot

One camper reported lying awake as something massive walked past his tent:

"You don't hear footsteps.

You *feel* them."

He said it sounded like a truck rolling over soft earth — but when he looked in the morning, there were no tire tracks and no footprints.

Just flattened moss in a pattern too wide to be human and too long to be a bear.

8. Are They Bigfoot? Or Something Bigger?

While some traits overlap with Bigfoot-type encounters, the giants described here are consistently:

- taller
- broader
- quieter
- more composed
- more territorial
- more inhuman

If the watchers and forest hominids represent one branch of Temagami's unknowns, the giants appear to be something else entirely:

A higher tier. Older, less curious, more aware, and tied to desolate areas.

Some Indigenous stories in the region speak of ancient forest guardians or *misikinabik*, beings older than time who protect the oldest places.

Some stories refer to them as "the Ancient Ones," who walk only at night.

Whatever they are, the giants appear not to approach humans with intent. They observe from distance, as if ensuring the deeper secrets of Temagami are not trespassed upon.

9. What the Giants Reveal About the Larger Pattern

Giants appear:

- near desolate places
- at the edges of deep lake trenches
- around cloaked-being hotspots
- on ridges bordering ancient cedars
- at sites of strange forest rearrangement
- on cliffs overlooking sky-light activity
- in areas where predators-that-aren't-bears retreat

They seem to operate at the **boundaries** of the mystery. Not inside it.

They are the **threshold keepers**.

Where the watchers observe, the giants defend.

Where the predators stalk, the giants stand sentinel.

Where the lake creatures rise from the dark, the giants appear at the waterline.

They are not enemies.

They are not hunters.

They are the old guardians of the hidden parts of Temagami.

And the next chapter takes us into the most terrifying aspect of all:

The beings that impersonate us.

CHAPTER 26 — THE MIMICS

Voices That Sound Like Friends, Footsteps That Match Your Own, and the Beings in Temagami That Imitate Us Too Well

1. When the Forest Speaks With Your Voice

There are things in Temagami that watch.Things that walk.Things that glide.Things that haunt.

And then there are things that **imitate**.

Not owls mimicking other owls.Not coyotes yipping like infants.Not loons echoing cries across the lake.

No — this is something else.

Witnesses describe:

- voices calling their name
- voices calling *in their own voice*
- the sound of a friend or partner asking for help
- footsteps matching their exact pace
- coughing from behind a tree
- laughter that sounds exactly like someone they know
- familiar whistles coming from the wrong direction

And here is the pattern:

These mimics never approach camp. They never step into the firelight. They never show themselves.

They imitate from just out of sight.

And they always do it when someone is alone.

2. The Man Who Heard His Own Voice Calling From the Trees

One of the most chilling encounters comes from a solo paddler who had pulled into a tiny cove to spend the night.

As he collected firewood, he heard someone call his name.

Not shouted. Not whispered. Just spoken in a calm, conversational tone:

"Daniel."

He froze.

The voice sounded exactly like his brother — same cadence, same warmth — except his brother was hundreds of kilometers away.

Then the voice called again:

"Daniel. Over here."

But the forest was empty.

Daniel later wrote:

"It wasn't just my brother's voice.

It was *perfect*.

Exactly right. And I don't know if that's what scared me or comforted me…

until it said my name again with no emotion at all."

The third time the voice called, it sounded flat, wrong, like someone repeating a recording without understanding tone.

Something in the woods was practicing.

3. The Friend Who Wasn't There

Two friends canoeing near Scarecrow Lake got separated during a brief storm.

When the rain cleared, one friend heard the other calling from the treeline:

"Come here! I found something!"

The voice was unmistakable. Same accent. Same enthusiasm.

The paddler shouted back but got no answer.

He stepped onto shore, walked toward the trees, and the voice called again:

"Over here! Hurry!"

He walked deeper, following his friend's voice… until he reached a clearing and realized:

There were **no footprints.** No sign his friend had ever been there. And the voice suddenly came from *behind him* — closer than before.

He sprinted back to the canoe.

Minutes later he found his friend paddling toward him from the opposite direction — the real friend — who had never left the water.

Whatever he had followed into the treeshad known exactly how the friend sounded.

4. The Sound of a Child Crying Near the Shore

A family camping on a peninsula heard a child crying near the water at 2 a.m.

Soft at first. Then louder. Then desperate.

The mother ran out of the tent before her husband could stop her.

The crying came from the shoreline.

She approached with a flashlight and saw nothing — just black water.

As she turned back toward the tent, the crying began again…

from the other side of the peninsula.

She later said:

"It wasn't a child.

It was something that wanted me to think it was a child."

And she never camped in Temagami again.

5. The Footsteps That Match Your Own

Several hikers describe a phenomenon where footsteps follow behind them...but not normally.

The steps:

- land exactly when they step
- pause when they pause
- accelerate when they accelerate
- stop when they turn around

One hiker described it perfectly:

"It wasn't following me.

It was *mirroring* me."

This mirroring behavior appears again and again.

Instead of being hunted, people feel imitated.

And many report a sensation that the mimicry is:

- studying
- practicing
- learning

- adjusting

As if whatever is making the sound is trying to understand human movement one step at a time.

6. The Laughter That Wasn't Human

Two forestry workers camping on a ridge heard laughter near their fire.

Not forest laughter — not coyote yips or loon calls.

Human laughter.

Except not quite.

It was:

- too abrupt
- too short
- too empty
- lacking breath or joy
- more like someone imitating laughter without understanding what laughter is

One worker said:

"It was like a child practicing how to laugh for the first time."

The laughter circled their campsite, always just beyond the tree line, never approaching.

It stopped instantly when they shined their flashlight.

Not faded. Not quieted.

Stopped as if someone flicked off a switch.

7. The Mimic That Learned Too Fast

This account comes from a Temagami guide who was teaching two young clients how to make loon calls by cupping their hands.

After each call, something in the forest answered.

At first it sounded like a loon. Then, like something trying to sound like a loon. Then, something half-loon, half-human.

By the fifth or sixth call, the answering call had changed dramatically.

It was sharper. More hollow. More human in tone.

He said:

"It didn't sound like a loon anymore.

It sounded like someone learning how we sound."

They left the area immediately.

8. Voices That Call From Impossible Places

Paddlers often report hearing mimicked voices from places no person could physically stand:

- from the center of lakes at night
- from treetops
- from inside dense underbrush
- from cliff faces
- from open water where no boats are
- from deep valleys with no access
- from the tops of ridges

One paddler described hearing her boyfriend call from the treetops:

"Help me!"

But he was in the tent behind her.

The treetops swayed slightly, but no shape moved within them.

9. The Purpose of Mimicry

Every tradition that mentions mimics — Indigenous stories, survival lore, modern wilderness encounters — warns of the same thing:

Mimics don't attack. They don't approach. They rarely show themselves.

They lure. They test. They coax.

The mimicry could be:

- curiosity
- hunting behavior
- territorial testing
- play
- misdirection
- an attempt to draw people into deeper forest

But one truth is clear:

Mimics use human familiarity as bait.

They know what we respond to:

- loved ones
- children
- our own voices
- our names
- the call for help
- the illusion of safety

That kind of intelligence is deliberate.

And deeply unsettling.

10. What the Mimics Mean in the Larger Pattern

The watchers observe. The cloaked ones hide. The predators stalk. The giants guard. The lake creatures lurk deep below. The sky lights hover above.

But mimics?

Mimics interact.

Not physically, but psychologically.

They:

- draw attention
- exploit emotion
- imitate trust
- lure people toward danger
- replicate our sounds with eerie accuracy
- demonstrate learning behavior

This makes them some of the most dangerous entities in the Temagami system — not because they attack, but because they manipulate.

And when you cross-reference mimic encounters with other phenomena, a shocking pattern emerges:

Mimic hotspots overlap directly with:

- missing time incidents
- vanishings
- desolate places
- giant sightings
- cloaked presences
- underwater creature zones
- lake hum activity

It's all connected.

Mimics sit at the junction of the psychological and the physical, the natural and the supernatural, the visible and the hidden.

They are the boundary-crossers.

The next chapter reveals what happens when these boundaries tighten — when everything in Temagami begins to line up into one coherent, terrifying structure.

CHAPTER 27 — THE SHAPE OF THE UNKNOWN
How Temagami's Disconnected Mysteries Begin to Form a Single, Terrifying Pattern

1. When Thirty Different Mysteries Start Whispering the Same Answer

For most of my life, Temagami felt like a thousand disjointed mysteries:

One person sees a giant. Another hears laughter from the treetops. Someone else witnesses a woman gliding through fog. Two paddlers see lights above a blackwater lake. A hunter finds a trail of massive footprints that stop in mid-snow. A family hears a child crying where no children exist.

Each event seemed isolated. Unrelated. Filed into its own mental drawer.

But as I gathered witness statements, mapped incidents, and compared locations, a slow unsettling truth began to take shape:

These things are not separate mysteries. They are fragments of the same one.

Temagami doesn't contain multiple phenomena.

Temagami contains **one system** expressing itself in different ways.

This chapter is where it begins to show its outline.

2. The Same Locations Keep Appearing

When you line up the maps — Bigfoot sightings, ghost activity, underwater creatures, sky lights, mimicry hotspots, desolate zones, vanished camps — the overlap is almost perfect.

The same locations appear again and again:

- deep-lake trenches
- ridge-lines with old growth
- narrow valleys where sound dies
- historic logging sites
- abandoned trapline corridors
- islands with collapsed cabins
- sharp elevation transitions
- places where the forest rearranges itself
- thin-place zones with unexplained cold air

Witnesses didn't talk to each other. Most never met. Many didn't even report their encounters until years later.

Yet they all experienced something in the same places.

The forest doesn't have random haunted spots. It has **nodes**.

Points of intensity.

Anchors.

3. The Behaviours Match Across Categories

What finally pushed me from "coincidence" to "pattern" was the behaviour.

Across every category of encounter:

- watchers
- cloaked presences
- giants
- lake creatures
- mimics
- camp hauntings
- sky lights
- desolate zones
- forest rearrangement
- screaming forest
- missing time

one trait appears again and again:

Intelligence.

Not human.Not animal.Not directional.

A single intelligence manifesting in multiple forms.

You see it in:

The watchers:

Observing from ridges.Not approaching.Deliberate pacing.

The giants:

Standing sentinel.Marking boundaries.

The mimics:

Learning voices.Testing responses.

The lake creatures:

Approaching silently.Matching canoe speed.

The sky lights:

Tracking people.Hovering above deep water.

The hauntings:

Residual, but aware.Responding to presence.

The desolate places:

Avoided by all living things.Holding empty space.

Across all of these phenomena, something larger is expressing itself in different layers of the environment.

Like different organs of the same creature.

4. The Vertical Ecosystem — Forest, Water, Sky

Through dozens of witness accounts, a vertical pattern emerges.

Above:

Lights — scanning, observing, gliding, descending.

At the surface:

Mimics, watchers, cloaked presences — intelligent interaction.

On the forest floor:

Predators-that-aren't-bears — territorial enforcers.

Deep in the water:

Massive creatures — ancient, silent, unrecorded.

Underground or in the voided places:

Desolate zones — something removed or dormant.

These layers operate like a **stacked ecosystem**, each level aware of the other, each performing a role.

Temagami is not a place with mysteries.

Temagami is a **multi-tiered living system of mysteries**.

The forest is the skin.The lakes are the lungs.The sky lights are the eyes.

And the giants —they feel like the bones.

5. The Boundary Signs

Another pattern emerged when I charted where people feel suddenly unwelcome.

There are recurring boundary markers:

- snapped trees at unnatural heights
- silence that falls abruptly
- sudden lack of bird activity
- moss that depresses strangely
- missing sections of trail
- campfire heat being pulled downward
- compasses spiraling
- voices fading abruptly
- shadows that retreat from certain zones

These aren't random signs.

They mirror what animals do when establishing territory:

- moose scrape trees

- wolves scent-mark boundaries
- bears rub their backs on trunks

But these boundary signs are different.

They feel like warnings.

Not "stay away" warnings.Not territorial warnings.

But **threshold warnings**.

As if the land is saying:

"Beyond this point, things change."

And witnesses confirm that when they cross these invisible lines, everything does change —the air,the sound,the sense of gravity,the behaviour of the unknown.

6. The Witnesses All Describe the Same Emotion

Across hundreds of accounts — your own included — the emotional reactions share the same pattern:

- pressure in the chest
- feeling "studied"
- sudden nausea
- dizziness at boundaries
- hair rising without cold wind

- gut-level dread
- strange calm
- a sense of being "beneath" something
- a feeling of stepping into an older world
- the sense of trespassing

One emotion appears more than any other:

Awe.

Not wonder.Not amazement.

Awe.

A mixture of fear, respect, and primal recognition that you are in the presence of something vast, ancient, and beyond the human world.

Temagami's unknowns aren't like typical cryptid stories.

They are **hierarchical.Systemic.Interwoven.**

The emotional signature suggests people are not encountering many creatures —they are encountering many faces of the same thing.

7. The Mimics Belong to the Same System

The mimics aren't random anomalies.

The fact that they appear in:

- desolate places
- deep lake edges
- giant sighting corridors
- cloaked-presence areas
- ancient cedar stands
- places where creatures rise or lights appear

proves something terrifying:

They are part of the system. A communicative arm. A psychological probe.

Mimicry is not a party trick. It's learning behaviour.

It's testing human boundaries.

And in the context of the entire Temagami web, mimics look like:

The forest's way of reaching out —without revealing itself.

8. The Forest Rearrangement Fits Too

The phenomenon where:

- camps reset
- objects move
- trails disappear
- signs vanish

- ground impressions erase overnight

once felt like a trickster ghost phenomenon.

But they align with the same pattern:

boundary enforcement and environmental manipulation.

Just like the giants guard physical boundaries and the mimics test psychological ones, the forest rearrangement maintains environmental boundaries.

It's not random.

It's governance.

9. All Roads Lead to the Center

When all the sightings, lights, sounds, desolate zones, and creature paths are mapped together, they form a disturbing shape:

A **ring** around a central region of Temagami.

A region almost no one enters. A region with no established camps. A region without trails. A region surrounded by desolate places like a moat.

Inside that center:

- underwater trenches
- ancient cedar giants
- inaccessible marshland
- steep ravines

- unusually frequent fog
- strange acoustics
- the highest concentration of sky lights
- missing hunters and canoeists
- no recorded Indigenous settlements
- no logging history
- extreme absence of wildlife

The shape is too deliberate to ignore:

Everything circles the same place.Everything avoids the same place.Everything emanates from the same place.

The watchers patrol the border.The giants stand guard.The mimics lure at its edges.The forest rearranges to hide it.The sky lights hover above it.The lake creatures rise from beneath it.

This is not random.This is **architecture**.

A structure built across land, water, and sky.

Something occupies Temagami's heart.

Not a creature.Not a ghost.Not a cryptid.

A **presence**.

Something with hierarchy, purpose, territory, intelligence, and ancient roots.

The shape of the unknown is not a beast.

It is a system.

A living, breathing, multi-layered intelligence spread across Temagami's terrain.

And the next chapter delves into its borders —the invisible barrier witnesses brush against without understanding:

CHAPTER 28 — TEMAGAMI'S INVISIBLE BOUNDARY

The Line You Can't See, Can't Measure, and Don't Know You've Crossed — Until the Forest Responds

1. There's No Signpost. No Marker. But Everyone Knows When They've Crossed It.

The boundary is real.

No map shows it. No sign warns you. No landmark signals its approach.

But almost every serious Temagami explorer has stepped across it at least once.

And every single one describes the same moment —that sudden, unmistakable feeling:

"We shouldn't be here."

Not lost. Not threatened. Not stalked.

Just wrong.

As if the world has subtly shifted in a way your body feels before your mind understands.

The boundary doesn't look like a line.

It feels like a line.

A shift in:

- air pressure
- silence
- emotional temperature
- animal presence
- the forest's awareness of you

Most never talk about it.Those who do can't describe it well.

But they all agree:

Something on the other side is older than the treesand deeper than the lakes.

2. The Sudden Silence — The First Signal You've Crossed Over

The most reliable indicator of the boundary is absolute silence.

Total.Immediate.Complete.

Birds stop singing.Insects stop buzzing.Wind seems to cut off mid-gust.

This isn't natural silence —the kind that slowly settles in before rain or after dusk.

This is a **switched-off** silence.

Witnesses describe:

- ears feeling "stuffed"
- voices sounding muffled
- boots making no echo
- breathing sounding too loud
- the world going flat

One paddler said:

"It was like someone turned the environment down to zero."

This silence never lasts long.

But it is the moment the boundary recognizes you.

3. The Line Animals Refuse to Cross

Dogs always sense it first.

Trail dogs that guide like professionals suddenly sit down and tremble.Sled dogs refuse to step forward.Well-trained hunting dogs flatten themselves against their owners' legs.

Even wild animals stop:

- moose halt mid-stride
- wolves circle wide
- deer turn abruptly
- beavers slap the water and vanish
- birds refuse to land

This isn't instinct or fear.

It's recognition.

One hunter described his dog's reaction:

"She froze.

Laid down.

Whimpered.

She wasn't scared of something in front of us—

she was scared of the place itself."

Predators avoid it.Prey avoid it.

Yet humans walk right in.

4. The Subtle Physical Symptoms People Report

A surprising number of witnesses describe similar physical sensations when they cross the boundary:

- pressure in the chest
- nausea at the base of the throat
- mild dizziness
- ears feeling "full"
- fingertips tingling

- a faint vibration in the legs
- heart rate increasing slightly
- the sense of being *lighter* or *heavier* without reason

Many compare it to altitude changes or sudden drops in air density.

One paddler said:

"It felt like stepping through a curtain made of static."

Another:

"As if the world behind me still existed,

but the world in front of me was older."

These sensations last seconds to minutes, but they always accompany boundary crossings.

5. The Forest Rearrangement Begins Near the Threshold

From earlier chapters, we know the forest rearrangement — moved objects, erased camps, altered trails — is not random.

The highest concentration of these events occurs directly along the boundary's edge.

This suggests the rearrangement phenomena serve a purpose:

- as warning signs
- as redirects

- as markers
- as corrections for human intrusion

One canoeist described walking a portage that seemed normal until it bent sharply around a boulder.Beyond that point, the moss became undisturbed,as though no human had ever walked there.

He later realized:

"I think the trail didn't end.

I think the forest moved it."

The boundary is not fixed.It shifts like a breathing thing.But its presence is constant.

6. Mimics and Watchers Are Most Active At the Edge

Almost every mimicry event in Temagami occurs along the boundary.

This is not coincidence.

It is behavior.

The mimics call out from just inside the invisible threshold.They use voices to lure, test, or warn.

Watchers — the hominid-type beings — are seen pacing along the boundary like patrols.

Their patterns are too consistent:

- they parallel paddlers
- they stay equidistant
- they never cross certain ravines
- they rarely enter desolate zones

One witness said:

"It felt like they were keeping us from going deeper.

Not hunting.

Just… blocking."

Another:

"Like guards on a border."

7. Giants Appear Only on the Boundary — Never Within It

In Chapter 26, we established the giants' role as threshold guardians.

Mapping sightings against boundary locations reveals a chilling truth:

Giants never appear inside the boundary. Only at its edge.

They are the tallest, strongest, and most territorial of Temagami's unknowns.

Yet even they do not cross whatever lies beyond.

They stop at:

- cliff edges
- lake drop-offs
- deep ravines
- cedar stands older than recorded history
- certain bogs where no birds land
- ancient fault lines

They stand facing the inner region.Watching.Waiting.

Almost protecting.

As though something behind them must not be disturbed.

8. Sky Lights Hover Above the Central Region

The aerial anomalies —hovering orbs, triangle lights, drifting spheres —do something no aircraft does:

They hover directly above the boundary interior.

Not randomly.Not occasionally.

Regularly.

Consistently.

Witnesses describe lights:

- descending close to the water
- scanning the treetops
- forming geometric patterns
- drifting over the central forbidden area
- rising vertically into the night sky
- disappearing silently

These lights don't behave like drones or meteorological phenomena. They behave like surveillance.

If the watchers and giants guard the boundary from the ground, the lights guard it from above.

9. Inside the Boundary — A Region Without Witnesses

This is the most disturbing part:

Almost no one has entered the boundary interior —and lived to describe what happened.

People skirt its edges. People walk into it briefly. People feel the shift. People back out instinctively.

But almost nobody goes deep inside.

Those who try:

- turn around

- get disoriented
- experience overwhelming dread
- encounter mimicry
- see giants watching from treelines
- hear screams from impossible distances
- lose hours
- vanish from maps temporarily
- or never speak of it afterward

A paddler whose GPS froze completely for hours on the boundary interior, only functioning again once she exited the zone.

Another report described **blinding white fog** that moved *against* the wind.

Another described hearing "hundreds of footsteps" moving in synchrony —from everywhere and nowhere.

Whatever is inside the boundary is not meant for human presence.

And every layer of Temagami's mystery— watchers, giants, mimics, forest rearrangement, lake entities, sky lights, dead zones —all point to one conclusion:

There is something in the center.

Something so old, so vast, and so integrated with the land that everything else exists to either protect it or hide it.

10. The Boundary Is Not to Keep Something Out —

It Is to Keep Something In**

When you look at the pattern as a whole:

- the watchers' patrols
- the giants' defensive stance
- the mimics' psychological lures
- the sky lights' circles
- the forest's living rearrangement
- the desolate zones acting as buffers

you realize something profoundly unsettling:

The boundary is not constructed to keep people **out**.

It is constructed to keep something **in**.

Something the land does not want released. Something that moves in ways we can't detect. Something tied to the ancient geology and the oldest waters. Something that has shaped Temagami since long before any canoe slipped across its lakes.

What the witnesses agree on —regardless of what they saw, or heard, or encountered.

CHAPTER 29 — WHAT THE WITNESSES AGREE ON

Thirty Chapters of Fragments, Hundreds of Eyewitnesses, Seasoned Field Researchers, and One Terrifying Consensus

1. Not Everyone Saw the Same Thing,

But Everyone — Including Field Researchers — Felt the Same Thing**

Temagami's mysteries come from every kind of wilderness traveler:

- hunters
- paddlers
- guides
- families
- Indigenous elders
- trappers
- forestry workers
- solo hikers
- police officers
- tourists

- and **field researchers**, the few who deliberately go into the deep bush seeking patterns instead of running from them

Their descriptions differ wildly:

Some saw giants.Some heard mimicry.Some watched lights hovering above lakes.Some saw ghostly workers in flooded cabins.Some felt a presence pacing their camp.Some heard inhuman screams echoing through valleys.Some witnessed shadows rising from underwater trenches.Some listened to footsteps that matched their own.Some felt the world "tilt" as if stepping through a membrane.

But despite all differences in encounter category,all distances,all backgrounds,all levels of wilderness experience…

everyone comes home describing the same core truth about Temagami.

Especially the field researchers —those who return again and againand recognize the patterns others miss.

2. Field Researchers Agree:

The Forest Is Aware In a Way That Shouldn't Be Possible**

You can dismiss the untrained eye.You can blame tourists for misidentifications.You can chalk up fear to inexperience.

But you cannot easily dismiss:

- researchers who have spent decades in the bush
- trackers who know the difference between bear trails and something else

- paddlers who have logged thousands of kilometers
- wildlife specialists who understand animal behavior
- sound analysts who record and study nocturnal calls
- people who deliberately set up audio, IR, thermal, and night-recording equipment

These individuals don't scare easily.

They don't exaggerate. And they don't jump to supernatural explanations.

Yet they say things like:

"It wasn't just an animal reacting to my presence.

It felt like the land itself was aware of me."

"Something studied the camp.

It wasn't curious.

It was evaluating."

"I'm not saying the forest is alive…

I'm saying it behaves like it is."

Field researchers rarely agree on terminology — but they agree on *sensation*:

Temagami behaves like a unified organism.

3. Even the Most Skeptical Researchers Admit:

The Watchers Aren't Animals**

Hunters and hikers sometimes mistake things. Field researchers don't.

They know:

- the sound of a bear snapping branches
- how moose walk
- how wolves move through underbrush
- what human pacing sounds like
- the difference between weight distribution on two legs and four
- what a stealthy animal sounds like vs. an observing one

And the watchers — the pacing ridgewalkers — behave in a way that defies comparison.

A veteran field researcher put it this way:

"It wasn't hunting me.

It was monitoring me.

That's not animal behavior.

That's *management* behavior."

Another researcher said:

"It shadowed us for forty minutes.

Same distance, same rhythm, same awareness.

That's not instinct.

That's policy."

When the people who know the land best agree that something deliberate walks these woods, you listen.

4. Field Researchers and Witnesses Are Unanimous on the Giants

No one — not hikers, paddlers, hunters, or researchers — has ever described giant behavior as random.

They don't:

- stalk
- chase
- roar
- threaten
- wander aimlessly
- enter camps

They appear exactly where the boundary begins.

And they keep their distance.

One researcher said:

"It stood on a ridge like a guard tower.

It didn't move.

It waited for us to leave."

Another:

"It wasn't a creature.

It was a sentinel."

Only field researchers, who map sightings and take detailed notes, notice something even more chilling:

Every giant sighting aligns perfectly with the perimeter of the forbidden interior region.

They are the outer wall.

The first line.

The silent sentinels of Temagami.

5. Mimics: Field Researchers Notice the Learning Behavior

Casual campers report voices.

But field researchers record patterns.

They've documented:

- mimicry improving over time
- voices becoming more accurate
- laughter learning cadence
- names pronounced with increasing precision
- footsteps growing more synchronized with the witness'

One seasoned researcher described hearing something imitate his own voice:

"It wasn't perfect.

But it was practicing."

Another:

"It called my name with the wrong emotion,

like someone reading a script they didn't understand."

Field researchers agree on one disturbing detail:

This is not an animal mimicking sound. It is an intelligence mimicking *communication*.

6. Ghost Encounters:

Researchers Say These Are Not Residual Hauntings**

Field investigators — both paranormal and biological — report the same thing:

Temagami's "hauntings" respond.

Not replay. Not loop. Not echo.

Respond.

A researcher who investigated the cabin-cook apparition described:

"It wasn't a ghost from the 1940s.

It was something acknowledging us —

intelligent, aware, and interacting."

Another:

"It felt like the forest was wearing a human memory

like a costume."

These aren't hauntings. These are **manifestations**.

Expressions of something deeper.

7. Lake Creatures and Lights:

Researchers Agree They're Connected**

People on the water see:

- massive shadows
- impossible silhouettes
- giant heads rising quietly

- something gliding beneath the canoe

People in the sky see:

- lights scanning the lake
- orbs hovering above deep basins
- shapes moving in geometric paths

Field researchers — who map both — see the truth:

The deep-water creatures and sky lights appear in the **exact same locations**.

The system is not horizontal.

It is **vertical**.

A pillar of activity rising from deep waterstraight into the night sky.

8. Desolate Zones:

Researchers Treat Them Like Radiation Zones**

Field researchers call these places:

- dead patches
- voids
- drains
- silent pockets

- null zones
- cold lungs
- hollow ground

Researchers consistently report:

- equipment malfunctions
- audio interference
- rapid temperature shifts
- drone instability
- GPS freeze
- chest pressure
- sudden fatigue
- emotional heaviness

These effects are not localized in one place —they form a ring around something deeper.

The boundary's outer membrane.

Researchers treat these zones the way scientists treat wildlife around Chernobyl:

With respect. With distance. With caution. And with the sense that the environment itself has changed at a fundamental level.

9. Researchers and Witnesses Alike Agree
—

Temagami's Boundary Is Real**

Almost every serious outdoors person has crossed it once.

And every field researcher has felt it.

Call it:

- the perimeter
- the line
- the quiet belt
- the ancient ring
- the old circle
- the hush zone
- the skin of something larger

They all describe the same moment:

"We passed through something."

Field researchers, who track these moments with precision, notice:

- silence spikes
- animal tracks vanish
- energy changes

- forest architecture shifts
- emotional state realigns
- intelligence in the forest becomes more present

This isn't imagination.

This is **pattern**.

10. The Final Consensus:

Everything Is Connected**

Across hundreds of accountsand dozens of seasoned field observers,there is one universal agreement:

Temagami is not a collection of creatures and ghosts.It is a single, interconnected intelligence expressing itself through the land.

A system.

A layered organism.

A multi-level presence.

Witnesses say:

"It understands us."

"It adapts."

"It warns."

"It manipulates the environment."

"It tests boundaries."

"It protects something."

"It is older than people."

"We walked inside something alive."

And the field researchers —the ones who measure, log, analyze, compare, return —summarize it best:

"It's not one phenomenon.

It's a unified system.

A forest intelligence we don't have a name for."

This is the final chapter of the mystery…but not the end of the story.

CHAPTER 30 — THE CONSISTENCY OF FEAR
Why Every Witness Carries the Same Quiet Terror Home From Temagami

1. Fear Has Many Shapes, But in Temagami It Has Only One Source

Fear normally varies from person to person.

A hunter's fear is different from a paddler's. A solo camper fears different things than a family. A field researcher fears danger in the data, not the dark.

But Temagami produces a different kind of fear:

a consistent fear — steady, unchanging, shared across witnesses who never met each other, never traded stories, and never compared notes.

This consistency is the single most important clue to understanding the wilderness intelligence described in this book.

People don't describe:

- panic
- hysteria
- terror

They describe something deeper:

Recognition.

As if some instinct locked deep inside the human mind wakes up in Temagami and whispers:

"We have been here before.

We remember this place.

This is older than us."

It's not fear of something happening.

It's fear of something **already here**.

2. The Fear Doesn't Arrive Quickly.

It Arrives Quietly.**

Most wilderness dangers are loud:

- A bear crashing through brush
- A moose snorting
- Wolves howling
- Rapids rising unexpectedly
- A storm sweeping over a ridge

But the fear in Temagami does not arrive like that.

It appears in stages, subtle as fog:

1. **You notice the forest listening.**

2. You feel watched but not threatened.

3. Sounds change — or stop altogether.

4. The land loses its familiarity.

5. Your body reacts before your mind does.

6. The fear settles into your bones like cold water.

One witness said:

"I didn't get scared.

I became aware."

Another:

"Nothing chased me.

Nothing screamed.

I just… knew I had gone too far."

It is fear without a predator.

Fear without a source.

Fear of a **threshold** crossed.

3. Field Researchers Feel It the Most — And Admit It the Least

You can always tell when someone has truly spent time in the deep bush.

They talk differently about fear.

Not in the frantic, high-adrenaline way city campers do.

Not in the humorous, shrug-it-off way experienced canoeists do.

Field researchers speak carefully about fear.Measured.Deliberate.

Almost respectfully.

One researcher said:

"I felt like the land was letting me in deeper than I deserved to go."

Another:

"The forest wasn't hostile.

It was warning me politely."

The most seasoned researchers — the ones who've heard the mumbling, mapped the hotspots, and stepped into dead zones — eventually confess something they don't put in their field notes:

"There's a point beyond which I won't go."

They don't say it dramatically.

They say it like someone acknowledging a universal truth.

4. The Fear Is Not Of What You See

But What Exists Just Outside of Sight**

Most encounters lie at the edge of perception:

- The watcher pacing at the ridge
- The giant standing at the cliff
- The mimic calling from the treeline
- The lake shape rising silently
- The cloaked figure flickering between trees
- The lights hovering above the basin
- The dead zone where no creature enters
- The scream layered with too many voices
- The fog that moves against the wind
- The footsteps that match your own

What terrifies people is not the creature or phenomenon itself.

It is the implication.

Something in Temagami operates at a scale and intelligence we are not equipped to understand.

And it chooses how close it comes.

Witnesses fear **the intention**, not the manifestation.

5. Fear Emerges From Patterns —

Not Single Events**

A single unexplained moment might scare you.

But patterns break you.

Witnesses describe fear setting in only when the pieces connect:

- The mimicry heard the night before
- The watcher seen earlier on the ridge
- The giant seen standing near the water
- The lake hum that accompanied both
- The desolate zone they unknowingly walked through
- The silence that arrived too suddenly
- The rearranged campsite they woke to

It is only when the puzzle pieces align that the true fear arrives:

This wilderness is organized.

Not random.Not chaotic.Not accidental.

Organized.

With rules.Boundaries.Behaviors.Structures.Roles.Layers.

People fear systemsmore than they fear individual creatures.

6. The Fear Is Consistent Because the Intelligence Is Consistent

Every type of phenomenon — watchers, giants, mimics, ghosts, lights, water creatures, desolate zones — follows the same logic:

- They respond, but rarely attack.
- They observe, but rarely pursue.
- They warn, but rarely harm.
- They appear, but rarely reveal themselves fully.
- They interact at the boundary, not the center.

This consistency across phenomena, locations, decades, and witnesses suggests one disturbing truth:

Temagami's intelligence is coordinated.

The watchers watch for a reason.The giants stand guard for a reason.The mimics lure and measure for a reason.The lake creatures rise where the lights descend.The desolate zones buffer something deeper.The forest rearranges itself to hide something older.The screams echo from a place we are not meant to reach.The boundary exists to contain, not exclude.

People fear what they cannot categorize.But they fear even more what they begin to understand —just enough to realize the structure is immense.

7. The Fear Stays With You —

Long After You've Left**

Witnesses describe the same lingering effects:

- The forest in their dreams
- The silence resurfacing in memory

- The feeling of not being alone
- A recurring sense of being watched
- Nightmares of walking into fog that parts around them
- A heaviness when thinking of going back
- A pull — both dread and curiosity

One paddler said:

"I left Temagami.

But Temagami didn't leave me."

Another:

"The fear doesn't fade.

It settles into you.

Not because of what happened…

but because of what could have happened."

Field researchers describe a different aftereffect:

"You come home and realize the world feels too small.

You've seen a system bigger than anything people talk about."

The fear transforms into respect.

And into truth.

8. The Final Truth Witnesses Agree On

After hundreds of accounts, decades of notes, countless maps, dozens of audio logs, and personal experiences that resurface at 3 a.m. when the house is silent…

Everyone —from frightened touriststo hardened huntersto lifelong paddlersto your fellow field researchers —agrees on one thing:

Temagami is alive.And it does not want to be understood.It wants to be respected.

Fear is not a flaw.

Fear is an instruction.

Fear is the language the wilderness useswhen something ancientwatches from the treelineand decides how close you may step.

Fear consistent across witnessesisn't panic.

It's truth.

A truth older than people,deeper than lakes,larger than giants,and brighter than the lights above the water.

The truth you now hold in your hands.

CHAPTER 31 — THE NIGHTS I COULD NOT EXPLAIN
My Own Encounters in the Temagami Wilderness, and Why I Keep Returning

1. Stepping Out From Behind the Reports

I've spent most of this book standing just outside the frame — telling other people's stories, cataloging other people's sightings, laying out the patterns that make Temagami one of the strangest wilderness regions in this country.

But the truth is simpler and harder:

I didn't write this book because I believed them. I wrote it because of what happened to me.

My own encounters are the reason I kept returning to Temagami, the reason I kept following up on old cases, and the reason this wilderness never loosened its grip on me. I didn't start out as a believer and I don't consider myself one now.

What I am — what I've always been — is someone who pays attention.

And Temagami gives you a lot to pay attention to.

2. The Road to Gull Lake — A Trail That Doesn't Want You There

My first personal experiences didn't start with anything supernatural. They started with a bad road.

The trail into the crown land campsite at **Gull Lake** is one of those Northern access routes that feels like it has a mind of its own. Even in a 4x4, you're fighting the terrain the entire way — axle-deep ruts, exposed granite, roots like knuckles punching up through the earth.

Trees lean in close enough to scrape the sides of the vehicle. It feels less like a road and more like a challenge.

A test.

Most people who camp there go once. Rarely twice. It's remote, hard to reach, and the silence hits differently.

But that road became the start of something I still think about years later.

3. The First Rock

The first night at Gull Lake, the forest was calm. Too calm.

I'd been sitting near the fire when a **rock landed about fifteen feet away**, heavy enough that it thudded instead of ticking off leaves. I didn't overreact. Rocks fall. Trees shed. The forest does weird things with gravity.

Then it happened again. And again. Each one landing closer, always from the same direction — the treeline just outside flashlight range.

You tell yourself it could be anything. You tell yourself it has to be.

Then you hear **footsteps**.

Soft at first. Then undeniably bipedal.

Slow, deliberate steps pacing the edge of the light, just far enough that I couldn't see anything except the movement of branches and the shifting texture of the dark.

It wasn't a moose. It wasn't a bear. It wasn't a drunk camper. There was no one else out there.

The pacing lasted long enough that I stopped pretending it was "nothing."

I stayed awake until the fire died. I didn't hear it leave.

4. The Tree Knocks — And the One That Hit Too Close

A few nights later, Gull Lake offered something different.

Around 11 p.m., a **series of distant tree knocks** echoed from somewhere across the water — clear, clean, spaced out like a code. I'd heard recordings of them for years, but hearing them in person is different. They vibrate in your ribs. They don't sound like something small striking wood.

They sound like communication.

I sat there listening, trying to figure out distance and direction, when a **single knock slammed against a tree behind me**, no more than thirty or forty feet away.

Violent. Sharp. Close.

Close enough that I stood up instantly.Close enough that the hair on my neck stood up with me.

It was the nearest thing to a warning I've ever felt in the bush.

Whatever made that sound was bigger than anything I wanted within arm's reach.I left the fire burning that night.

I didn't sleep much.

5. A Different Lake, A Different Kind of Night

Years later, I had another encounter, this time on a **small unnamed lake**, one of those quiet places that looks peaceful until the sun goes down. On this particular trip, the main problem wasn't anything strange.

It was bears.

A mother bear with **three yearling cubs** had discovered my camp — too curious, too bold, too accustomed to human presence. They wandered through like they owned the place. I chased them off, made noise, stood tall, did everything you're supposed to do.

But they kept coming back.Every half hour.Then every ten minutes.

Eventually, another **large black bear** showed up on top of it all, which is the point where you stop pretending you're in control of anything.

I ended up sitting in my SUV with the windows cracked, monitoring the campsite in the dark, listening to the bears breathe and huff and circle. It was one of those nights where wildlife demands your full attention.

Then something else entered the picture.

6. The Vocalization That Changed Everything

Around midnight, from somewhere in the dark timber about a hundred feet away, came a **deep, rising vocalization**.Not a bear.Not a wolf.Not a moose.

The bears reacted instantly.

All four of them — mother and cubs — stopped sniffing the campsite and **froze**. Their heads turned toward the sound in perfect unison.

Then, without hesitation, they **bolted**.

Not wandered away.Not trotted.They ran like their lives depended on it, crashing through the bush in the opposite direction.

If a sound scares a black bear that badly, you don't need an encyclopedia of wildlife biology to know something is off.

I stayed in the vehicle.

I wasn't going out there.

7. The Footsteps and the Mumbler

The rest of the night didn't calm down.

With the bears gone, something else took their place — **footsteps** again, circling the site.Slow.Heavy.Consistent.

At one point, around 3 a.m., I heard something that still gives me a cold feeling when I think about it:

A low, rolling **mumbling** — half speech, half vocal noise, coming from somewhere behind the fire ring.

It didn't sound like a person.It didn't sound like an animal.

It sounded like something trying to speak quietly to itself.

I'd heard reports of the "mumbling phenomenon" for years.I never thought I'd hear it myself.

That was the night I slept in the SUV.Even then, I barely slept at all.

8. The Morning After

At sunrise, I launched the drone and scanned the entire area. The only animals I spotted were **two of the cubs** further down the lake.

No mother.No large bear.

And nothing else.Nothing that explained the vocalization.Nothing that accounted for the pacing.

The forest had erased all signs.

It does that.

9. Why I Wrote This Book

People sometimes ask why I spend so much time on this — why I chase old reports, interview witnesses, and go into areas where most people would rather not spend a single night.

The answer isn't complicated:

I've heard the footsteps. I've seen the reactions of wildlife. I've felt the presence of something watching.

Temagami is not a place where stories fade. It's a place where the land itself feels like it's holding something back — not maliciously, not aggressively, but with a kind of old patience.

Writing this book wasn't about proving anything. It wasn't about convincing skeptics or converting believers.

It was about documenting a pattern that many people whisper about but rarely put into words.

It was about giving shape to experiences — mine, yours, the witnesses across decades — that deserve to be treated with seriousness.

I don't claim to know exactly what's out there.

But I know what I heard. I know what I felt. I know what the bears ran from.

And I know one thing above all:

Temagami is not done revealing itself.

APPENDIX A — Encounter Classification Index

A Field Researcher's Catalogue of Witness Reports from the Temagami Wilderness

Across Temagami and the surrounding northern wilderness, encounter reports fall into several recognizable patterns. While each incident is unique, the behaviours, environmental cues, and witness experiences overlap strongly enough to form reliable categories.

These categories are not meant to "solve" the mysteries of Temagami. They exist to **capture the diversity of encounters**, help researchers recognize patterns, and allow future readers to compare their own experiences.

This appendix is organized into the following major sections:

1. **Hominid Encounters**
2. **Giant-Type Encounters**
3. **Mimicry Phenomena**
4. **Cloaked / Partially Visible Entities**
5. **Predator-Type Unknowns**
6. **Forest Rearrangement Events**
7. **Desolate Zone Experiences**
8. **Ghost and Haunting-Type Encounters**

9. Lake & Underwater Entities

10. Sky Lights & Aerial Phenomena

11. Auditory Anomalies

12. Environmental / Psychological Distortion Events

13. Missing Time & Boundary Crossings

14. Multi-Phenomenon Composite Encounters

Each section contains:

- **Definition**
- **Behaviour Profile**
- **Notable Traits**
- **Witness Patterns**
- **Example Reports** (summarized)
- **Possible Interpretations**

1. HOMINID ENCOUNTERS (Standard "Watcher" Type)

Bipedal, intelligent, and often observed pacing or shadowing humans.

Definition: Large, upright, human-shaped figures 7–9 feet tall, often referred to as "watchers" or "ridge-walkers."

Behaviour Profile:

- Keep distance (30–150 meters)
- Walk parallel to witnesses
- Avoid direct confrontation
- Appear curious but cautious
- Observed flipping large logs, pacing ridges, or standing at treeline

Notable Traits:

- Heavy footsteps
- Silhouettes wider than human
- Rare vocalizations (deep, resonant sounds)
- High intelligence inferred from positioning

Common Witness Descriptions:

- "It kept pace with us without ever showing itself fully."
- "It watched, not hunted."

Example Reports:

- Ridge-walker shadowing canoeists near Wolf Lake
- A watcher pacing hunters for 40 minutes on an unnamed ridge

Interpretation: Likely part of a territorial or observational system.

2. GIANT-TYPE ENCOUNTERS (10–12+ Feet Tall)

Massive beings seen standing guard at boundary zones.

Definition: Extremely large, upright figures often 10–12 feet tall or more.

Behaviour:

- Stationary stance
- Guard-like posture
- Observed on cliffs, ridges, and at water edges
- Never approach camps

Notable Traits:

- Snapping trees 5–6 feet off the ground
- Ground tremors with each step
- Shoulders as wide as cedar trunks

Witness Pattern:

- "It didn't move. It waited."
- "It stood like a sentinel."

Interpretation: Boundary guardians or territorial markers.

3. MIMICRY PHENOMENA

Voices, footsteps, or laughter imitating humans.

Definition: Imitation of human sounds — often disembodied and unsettling.

Forms of Mimicry:

- Calling names
- Imitating family members
- Copying footsteps exactly
- Child crying near shorelines
- Laughter without emotion

Notable Traits:

- Direction changes abruptly
- Sounds come from impossible positions
- Mimicry improves with repetition

Example Witness Lines:

- "It used my brother's voice — perfectly."
- "The crying moved to the other side of the peninsula."

Interpretation: Learning behaviour; psychological probing.

4. CLOAKED / PARTIALLY VISIBLE ENTITIES

Semi-transparent, shimmering, or "predator-like" distortions.

Definition: Figures seen as distortions, blurs, or shimmering outlines.

Behaviour:

- Follow silently
- Vanish instantly
- Appear near desolate places
- Avoid direct light

Witness Patterns:

- "It was invisible but there."
- "A heat-haze shape of something big."

Interpretation: Possibly connected to boundary shifts.

5. PREDATOR-TYPE UNKNOWN BEINGS

Large forest entities that move without typical animal behavior.

Definition: Huge shapes moving like predators but lacking identifiable traits.

Traits:

- Quiet movement
- Heavy, deliberate steps
- Presence of dread
- Shadow-like motion

Example:

- "Something big matched our pace but sounded wrong for a bear."

Interpretation: Guard or enforcer-type species.

6. FOREST REARRANGEMENT EVENTS

Objects, camps, or natural elements shifted overnight.

Definition: Movement of items, trails, or campsite structures.

Forms:

- Gear repositioned
- Logs moved
- Trails erased

- Camps reset
- Fire pits rearranged

Notable Traits:

- No tracks
- No signs of human tampering
- Occurs overnight

Interpretation: Territorial regulation or environmental correction.

7. DESOLATE ZONE EXPERIENCES

Areas of complete silence, nausea, and emotional suppression.

Definition: Dead zones with no wildlife or sound.

Symptoms:

- Silence "shutting off"
- Chest pressure
- Nausea
- Dizziness
- Emotional dread

Witness Pattern:

- "The silence was switched off."

Interpretation: Boundary buffering zones or environmental anomalies.

8. GHOST & HAUNTING-TYPE ENCOUNTERS

Apparitions, phantom footsteps, disembodied workers.

Types:

- Cabin cook apparition
- Horse-drawn wagon heard but not seen
- Woman gliding across water
- Footsteps circling tents
- Breathing inside tents or cabins

Traits:

- Appear interactive
- Not residual replay
- Acknowledge presence
- Disappear without pattern

Interpretation: Manifestations of memory, consciousness, or forest expression.

9. LAKE & UNDERWATER ENTITIES

Massive shapes beneath canoes or rising to surface silently.

Forms:

- Enormous silhouettes
- Quiet ascents
- Canoes rocked without wind
- Water bulging upward

Notable Traits:

- Multi-ton mass
- No splashing
- Often accompanied by deep hums

Interpretation: Ancient aquatic species or deep under-lake anomalies.

10. SKY LIGHTS & AERIAL PHENOMENA

Orbs, triangles, descending lights, scanning motions.

Forms:

- Hovering above lake trenches
- Slow geometric movement
- White or amber spheres
- Beams directed at water

Notable Traits:

- Silent
- No wind disturbance
- Not drones or aircraft

Interpretation: Surveillance-like behaviour; tied to lake anomalies.

11. AUDITORY ANOMALIES

Sounds that defy source, physics, or direction.

Types:

- Bipedal footsteps without origin
- Metallic ringing deep in forest
- Multi-layered screams
- Echoes in non-echoing areas
- Whispers with no source

Patterns:

- Direction shifts
- Volume anomalies
- Voices repeating wrong tone

Interpretation: Environmental resonance or non-physical sound source.

12. ENVIRONMENTAL / PSYCHOLOGICAL DISTORTION EVENTS

Shifts in perception, air density, and emotional temperature.

Symptoms:

- "Static air"
- Warped time perception
- Color desaturation
- Sensation of gravity change
- Emotional flattening or intensification

Interpretation: Crossing thresholds into older ecological or energetic zones.

13. MISSING TIME & BOUNDARY CROSSINGS

Periods of lost hours or stepping into "other-feeling" spaces.

Markers:

- GPS malfunction
- Memory gaps
- Sudden fog
- Light changes
- Feeling of stepping into a different world

Interpretation: Interaction with deeper interior region or unknown phenomenon.

14. MULTI-PHENOMENON COMPOSITE ENCOUNTERS

Events involving two or more phenomena at once.

Examples:

- Sky lights above lake creatures
- Mimics at desolate boundaries

- Giants near rearranged forest zones
- Cloaked beings + watchers
- Ghostly apparitions + mimicry
- Missing time + deep hums

Interpretation: High-intensity nodes; possible interior boundary breaches.

Conclusion

This appendix provides a framework for understanding the diversity and interconnected nature of Temagami's unexplained encounters. While each category stands alone, together they form a cohesive system — an ecosystem of the unknown.

APPENDIX B — CHRONOLOGICAL LIST OF REPORTS & CASE FILES

A Historical Timeline of Sightings, Encounters & Unexplained Events in the Temagami Wilderness

This appendix provides a master chronological index of the most significant encounters, sightings, disappearances, auditory anomalies, and unexplained wilderness events in the Temagami region and surrounding northern districts. It includes modern cases (some ongoing), historical reports, Indigenous oral traditions, and long-standing backcountry accounts that have shaped Temagami's reputation as one of Ontario's most mysterious wilderness areas.

PRE-1900 — ANCIENT & EARLY INDIGENOUS ACCOUNTS

Pre-Contact Era – Anishinaabe Traditions

- Stories referencing *other-than-human beings* inhabiting cliffs, deep lakes, and old-growth pine stands.

- Warnings about certain islands where people "did not sleep," and where the forest behaved differently.

- Accounts of **Memegwesi** (Little People) seen near rivers and portage trails.

- Descriptions of **ridge watchers**—tall, silent figures appearing at dusk and vanishing instantly.

1600s–1800s — Early Guides, Trappers & Fur-Trade Observations

- Reports of **deep lake roars** at night with no wind present.
- Night footsteps around isolated campsites.
- **Shadow figures** witnessed standing on island points.
- Canoes followed quietly by **wandering lights** drifting across black water.
- Hunters hearing **children's voices** in regions with no settlements.

1900–1950 — THE EARLY WRITTEN PERIOD

1903 — Cliff Echo Voices (Lady Evelyn Region)

A trapper traveling beneath a granite face reported clear "voices in the stone."

1906–1970 — The Old Yellow Top Era (Cobalt & Temagami Fringe)

A legendary Bigfoot-type creature with a **distinct yellow patch of hair** was seen multiple times:

- **1906** — Miners witnessed an 8–foot creature with dark hair and a yellow crown.
- **1923** — Settlers saw it near a cattle line.

- **1947** — A school bus driver reported a tall, yellow-topped figure crossing the road.
- **1970** — Mine workers witnessed the creature near the Cobalt Lode Mine.

1912 — Ridge Silhouette (Maple Mountain)

Surveyors observed a pale, upright silhouette that disappeared without sound.

1928 — Island Footstep Case (Lake Temagami)

Canoeists heard bipedal pacing around their island camp; no tracks found.

1934 — Sharp Rock Light Phenomenon

White lights drifted between tree lines on a windless night.

1947 — Whispering Pines Case (Obabika Old Growth)

Witnesses heard "whispering like language" inside dense pine stands.

1950–1990 — THE MODERN ENCOUNTER ERA

1952 — Swimming Creature Report (Central Lake Temagami)

Two men watched a dark mass cross a bay "faster than any bear could swim."

1959 — Two Loud Slaps (Fergusson Island Cabin)

A cabin was struck hard twice at 2 AM; no wildlife observed.

1967 — Disappearance of Two Paddlers (Cross Lake)

Camp intact. Fire still warm. No sign of departure.

1971 — The Maple Mountain Watcher

A shadowy figure stood perfectly still on a skyline bluff for over twenty minutes.

1979 — Diamond Lake Pressure Wave Incident

A large underwater mass passed beneath an aluminum boat without surfacing.

1985 — Water Column Distortion (Sharp Rock Drop-Off)

A vertical mist column rose from still water and vanished instantly.

1989 — Whispering Portage (Wakimika to Diamond)

Brothers heard their names called repeatedly on a moonless night.

1990–2010 — THE INTENSIVE PATTERN YEARS

1991 — Temagami River Screamer

Groups along the river heard a long, chest-deep howl not matching any known species.

1994 — Island Cabin Pacer (South Arm)

Heavy footsteps circled a cabin for three consecutive nights.

1998 — The "Behind You" Voice Case (Wolf Lake)

Campers heard voices speaking directly behind them with no visible source.

2001 — Cross Lake Two-Camp Disappearance

Two separate camps discovered abandoned days apart; all gear intact.

2003 — Starfield Blackout Night (Fergusson Island)

Witnesses saw stars disappear in a large oval overhead for 15 seconds.

2006 — Underwater Shadow Pursuit (Diamond Lake)

A dark mass followed a canoe silently for over 200 meters.

2009 — Obabika Whistling Incident

Clear whistles from multiple directions; no visible movement.

2010 — Cabin Knock Mimic (Sharp Rock Outpost)

Knocks on windows followed by an identical "reply knock" from behind the cabin.

2010 — Rabbit Lake Cabin Incident (Veteran Hunters)

Growls, screams, pacing, and several cabin slaps. Family fled after two sleepless nights.

2010–PRESENT — CONTEMPORARY ENCOUNTERS & ACTIVE HOTSPOTS

2011 — Lake Temagami, July 22 — Growls & Screams

A family recorded deep growling and screaming sounds; phone interview conducted with Ontario Bigfoot.

2011 — Ridge Walker Photo (Maple Mountain)

A silhouette was photographed at sunset; no tracks found nearby.

2013 — Breath Against Tent (Temagami River)

A deep, resonant exhale woke two campers at once.

2014 — Rabbit Lake Screams (NE Timiskaming District)

Multiple reports of nighttime screams; two witnesses independently described the same pitch shifts.

2014 — Wilson Lake Vocals (Temagami Region)

Unexplained nighttime vocalizations recorded by campers.

2015 — Water Approach Entity (Lake Temagami)

A "floating log" approached shore, then rose and moved unnaturally before submerging.

2016 — Cabin Vibration Event (Fergusson Island)

Cabin shook twice around 4 AM; no wind or seismic activity recorded.

2017–Present — The Temagami Hunting Family Cases (West Temagami)

A hunting family has experienced **multiple encounters** over several seasons, including:

- Long stride tracks
- Heavy biped pacing
- Tree breaks
- Whistles and mimicry
- Dark figures observed between treesThis remains one of **Ontario Bigfoot's primary long-term active research areas**.

2018 — Island Rock Footsteps (Southwest Channels)

Distinct bipedal footsteps recorded on exposed granite; no prints visible.

2019 — Obabika Whisper Event

Murmuring voices grew louder then abruptly stopped.

2020 — Moose Panic (Diamond Lake Basin)

Two moose fled shallow water violently, seemingly reacting to something below the surface.

2021 — Full Silent Drop (Lake Temagami)

Forest silence hit abruptly for 70 seconds; followed by distant, deliberate knocking.

2022 — Shadow-Cliff Traverse (Lady Evelyn)

A tall silhouette crossed an exposed cliff face in complete silence.

2023 — Canoe Scrape Event (Sharp Rock)

A deep, slow scrape passed beneath two paddlers at night.

2024 — Night Visitor Slap Case (Central Temagami)

Cabin wall struck three times; soft sighing heard afterward.

2025 — Whisperer-Uptick Summer

Multiple reports of name-calling mimicry across several Temagami lakes.

NOTABLE THEMATIC PATTERNS ACROSS DECADES

1. Tall Forest Figures

1930s → present Seen on ridges, shorelines, and islands.

2. Whisper & Mimic Phenomena

1940s → present Portages & old-growth corridors.

3. Aquatic Disturbances

1950s → present Diamond, Obabika, Sharp Rock, and deep bays of Lake Temagami.

4. Cabin & Tent Pacing

1920s → present Islands, peninsulas, and remote cabins.

5. Dead-Silence Events

Consistent across all decades.

6. Disappearances With Intact Camps

Rare but disturbingly consistent.

SUMMARY

This chronological list reveals a striking truth:

Temagami's mysteries are not new. They are persistent. They are patterned. They are evolving. And they occur across every generation of witness who has entered these forests.

From ancient Indigenous oral history to modern audio recordings, the story does not change — only the witnesses do.

APPENDIX C — TEMAGAMI MYSTERY HISTORIC HOTSPOTS

A Guide to the Region's Strangest, Most Notorious Locations

Temagami is vast — thousands of lakes, hundreds of portages, endless forest. You can spend a lifetime exploring it and still never touch the true edges of the mystery.

But certain places…certain pockets of land and water…come up again and again.

Places where patterns form. Where sightings cluster. Where energies shift. Where paddlers, rangers, loggers, campers, and hunters all agree:

"Something happens out there."

These are the hotspots.

1. Lake Temagami — The Outer Channels

Bigfoot • Night Visitors • Island Disturbances

Region: Central Temagami Core**Known For:**

- Large, bipedal shapes pacing shorelines
- Nighttime cabin visitors
- Swimming "log-shaped" creatures

- Knocks, booms, and cabin wall slaps
- Mysterious footprints on islands

Why It's a Hotspot: Lake Temagami has hundreds of islands, most uninhabited. Creatures — whatever they are — have endless escape routes. The massive underwater trenches add a layer of aquatic mystery.

Witness Types:

- Families at camps and rentals
- Experienced paddlers
- Rangers
- Fishing guides

Unique Feature: Bigfoot-like creatures have been seen **swimming between islands**.

Danger Level: ★★★★☆ Not predatory, but very close-range encounters happen here.

2. Obabika Lake & the Ancient Forest

Spirits • Voices • Footsteps in Old Growth

Region: West Temagami **Known For:**

- Whispering voices between towering pines
- Ancient forest shadows that move on their own

- Sub-surface lake disturbances
- Light anomalies

Why It's a Hotspot: Home to the largest old-growth red and white pine stands in the region. Indigenous communities have long warned that the forest "remembers everything."

Witness Types:

- Backcountry paddlers
- Old-growth hikers
- Spiritual trekkers

Unique Feature: Nighttime whispers that sound like children or women far away — but come from nowhere.

Danger Level: ★★★★☆ Psychological danger is high. People have fled camps at night.

3. Lady Evelyn–Smoothwater Wilderness Area

Disappearances • Camps Left Intact • Ghost Lights

Region: Northeast of Temagami **Known For:**

- Campsites where hikers vanished without disorder
- Strange circular disturbance rings
- Lights floating low in valleys

- Long-distance vocalizations

Why It's a Hotspot: Extremely remote and difficult to access. Minimal human traffic. Natural amphitheater landscapes amplify sounds.

Witness Types:

- Veteran paddlers
- SAR teams
- Park rangers

Unique Feature: Multiple cases of **fires still burning** with their campers missing.

Danger Level: ★★★★★ This is the region with the most disappearances.

4. Maple Mountain Ridge

Ghost Figures • Ridge Walkers • Lights on Peaks

Region: Southeast of Smoothwater **Known For:**

- Tall pale figures standing on skyline ridges
- Lights drifting on the mountain at night
- Heavy footsteps without visible source
- "Ridge hum" vibrations reported by hikers

Why It's a Hotspot: One of the highest points in Ontario with deep spiritual history. Indigenous Elders consider the ridge a sacred vantage.

Witness Types:

- Hikers
- Canoeists who camp below
- Fire tower restoration volunteers

Unique Feature: Shadow figures appear repeatedly in the same locations.

Danger Level: ★★★☆☆ No aggression, but the area radiates strong presence.

5. Temagami River & the White Bear Forest Corridor

Night Screams • Heavy Footprints • Running Shadow Beasts

Region: South-Central Temagami **Known For:**

- Howls too deep for wolves
- Bipedal footsteps splashing upriver
- Massive silhouettes running ridge to ridge
- Tree breaks

Why It's a Hotspot: Old growth meets river channels — prime travel pathways for wildlife *and something else*.

Witness Types:

- Hikers
- Local cabin owners
- Hunters

Unique Feature: Something has been seen **running in the river**, upright, in thigh-deep water.

Danger Level: ★★★★☆ Fast-moving encounters, often aggressive-sounding vocalizations.

6. Cross Lake & The Eastern Peninsulas

Footsteps Without Tracks • Vanishing Camps • Blank Silence

Region: East of Lake Temagami **Known For:**

- Two missing campers (2001)
- Perfectly intact camps with no sign of departure
- Audible footsteps around tents with zero footprints
- Sudden dead-silence events

Why It's a Hotspot: Cross Lake holds deep cold pockets and narrow ridges that trap sound.

Witness Types:

- Canoe trippers
- Local fishing groups
- Search and rescue teams

Unique Feature: Circular patterns found in pine needles around tents.

Danger Level: ★★★★★ One of the highest-strangeness areas in Temagami.

7. Diamond Lake & Sharp Rock Inlet

Large Aquatic Shape • Canoe Impacts • Underwater Pulses

Region: North Temagami **Known For:**

- Something enormous moving below canoes
- Sub-surface shadows
- Pressure-wave hits from below
- Sudden bubbles rising in straight lines

Why It's a Hotspot: Deep-water trenches with abrupt drop-offs — prime habitat for unknown aquatic species.

Witness Types:

- Anglers

- Experienced canoeists
- Long-time lake residents

Unique Feature: Aluminum canoes have been **scraped from below** with deep gouges.

Danger Level: ★★★☆☆ Terrifying but not physically harmful — yet.

8. Wolf Lake Area

Night Whistles • Tree Peels • Children's Voices

Region: South of Lady Evelyn-Smoothwater **Known For:**

- Unexplained whistling patterns
- Tree bark peeled at impossible heights
- Reported child-like laughter
- Blue-white orbs moving low across rock faces

Why It's a Hotspot: This region has some of the oldest exposed rock and mineral-rich terrain — a magnet for strange atmospheric effects.

Witness Types:

- Climbers
- Canoe trippers
- Youth camps

Unique Feature: Voices repeating campers' names from the treeline.

Danger Level: ★★★★☆ Psychological disturbances reported frequently.

9. The Deep Bays of Fergusson Island

Shadow Forms • Drifting Canoes • Cabin Pacing

Region: Lake Temagami **Known For:**

- Figures moving between trees at dusk
- Canoes bumping shore without wind
- Heavy pacing around cabins
- Windows tapped repeatedly in the early morning

Why It's a Hotspot: Fergusson Island is large, heavily forested, and rarely fully explored.

Witness Types:

- Cabin renters
- Anglers
- Canoe route paddlers

Unique Feature: A recurring phenomenon of **tapping on windows** with no tracks outside.

Danger Level: ★★★☆☆ High adrenaline events but rarely harmful.

10. The Portage Between Diamond Lake & Wakimika Lake

Voices • Footsteps Behind Hikers • Echoes That Aren't Echoes

Region: Northwest Temagami**Known For:**

- Voices calling from behind
- Footsteps pacing hikers
- Shadows disappearing behind boulders
- Repeated "name-calling" phenomenon

Why It's a Hotspot: The portage travels through dense cedar swamp and high boulder ridges — perfect for acoustic distortions, or something mimicking them.

Witness Types:

- Solo hikers
- Groups finishing long loops
- Veteran paddlers

Unique Feature: Voices sounding identical to friends who are **nowhere near** the trail.

Danger Level: ★★★★☆ People have abandoned trips after a single crossing.

11. Nasmith Creek Backcountry

The Screamer • Bone Piles • Sudden Loss of Wildlife Sounds

Region: Western Temagami **Known For:**

- Bloodcurdling screams
- Fresh bone piles that weren't there the day before
- Forest going dead-silent without warning
- Shadow movement paralleling trails

Why It's a Hotspot: Brutal terrain with almost no human presence — perfect for large predators or unknown species.

Witness Types:

- Hunters
- Bushcrafters
- Long-range solo paddlers

Unique Feature: Screams that carry for miles but have no clear source.

Danger Level: ★★★★★ Highly intimidating, often triggers fight-or-flight.

12. Sharp Rock Access Road & Trails

Night Crossings • Roadside Figures • Eyeshine at Human Height

Region: East Temagami**Known For:**

- Tall figures crossing the access road at night
- Amber eyeshine in pairs
- Something walking parallel to cars
- Deep tree knocks in the valley

Why It's a Hotspot: This corridor connects multiple deep bays and ridges — a natural funnel for wildlife and unknown entities.

Witness Types:

- Drivers
- Camp staff
- Hunters

Unique Feature: Something has been seen pacing vehicles at running speed.

Danger Level: ★★★★☆ Close-range sightings are common.

APPENDIX D — TEMAGAMI CREATURE TYPES & BEHAVIORAL PATTERNS

A Field-Research Breakdown of the Unknown Entities Reported Across the Temagami Wilderness

Temagami doesn't have one mystery. It has many.

But after decades of testimonies — rangers, guides, families, paddlers, hunters, researchers, and longtime locals — patterns emerge. Distinct shapes. Distinct behaviors. Distinct "types" of encounters that repeat themselves across years, locations, and witnesses who never spoke to one another.

This appendix organizes those patterns into **eight major categories**, representing the strongest recurring themes.

These aren't species. They aren't "confirmed." They are **field-observed archetypes** — recurring forms of the unknown.

1. THE TALL FOREST WALKERS

(Bigfoot-Type Entities)

Common Regions: Lake Temagami islands, White Bear Forest, Lady Evelyn area, Wolf Lake corridor**Typical Height:** 7–10 feet**Notable Behaviors:**

- pacing cabins
- watching from ridges

- tree breaks at shoulder height
- swimming across bays at night
- slow, heavy footsteps circling camps
- slapping cabins or tents (territorial)

These are the classic "giants of the bush," consistently reported for more than 60 years.

Key Characteristics:

- Upright, massive, heavily built
- Dark fur (brown or black most common)
- Minimal vocalization
- Strong curiosity toward camps
- Rare direct aggression

Unique Pattern: More likely to be seen **swimming** in Temagami than in any other region of Ontario.

2. THE RIDGE SHADOWS

(Silent, Tall, Thin Figures Seen on Ridges)

Common Regions: Maple Mountain ridge, Obabika Old Growth, Cross Lake east ridge**Typical Height:** 6–9 feet**Appearance:**

- pale, thin silhouettes

- unmoving for long periods
- no visible facial details

Behaviors:

- stand motionless on skyline ridges
- appear closer each night
- vanish instantly when clouds obscure the moon
- sometimes sway subtly, like moving with unseen wind

Unique Pattern: Often associated with **a low hum or vibration** felt through the ground.

3. THE NIGHT VISITORS

(Cabin Prowlers, Tent Circlers, Window Knockers)

Common Regions: Temagami Island cabins, Sharp Rock inlet, Fergusson island bays**Behaviors:**

- pacing around structures
- tapping windows
- softly brushing against cabin walls
- leaning weight into buildings
- breathing beside tents

Often mistaken for bears — until the movement becomes too controlled.

Key Traits:

- Completely silent approach
- Bipedal pacing
- Leaves depressions or footprints in moss
- Withdraws when yelled at or confronted

Unique Pattern: Striking cabin walls with an open-palm "slap" — a common behavior in Temagami.

4. THE WATER-DWELLING SHAPES

(Sub-Surface Aquatic Phenomena)

Common Regions: Lake Temagami trenches, Obabika basin, Diamond Lake, Sharp Rock drop-offs **Behaviors:**

- rising beneath canoes
- bumping or scraping hulls
- creating perfect circular currents
- emitting deep underwater pulses
- breaking surface in brief, massive "shoulder rolls"

Not fish. Not logs. Not sturgeon.

Witnesses describe something large, smooth, and alive.

Unique Pattern: Shadowy masses bigger than canoes drifting silently under the surface.

5. THE WHISPERERS & MIMICS

(Auditory Entities)

Common Regions: Wolf Lake area, narrow cedar portages, Obabika Old Growth, Cross Lake trails**Behaviors:**

- voices calling names from the treeline
- whispers directly behind campers
- giggles or laughter in still air
- mimicry of known voices
- faint conversation-like murmuring

No visible form. Purely sound-based encounters.

Unique Pattern: Whispers often stop the moment someone turns their head — but start again when facing away.

6. THE SHORELINE SHAPE-SHIFTERS

(Creatures Mistaken for Logs, Rocks, or Low Shadows)

Common Regions: Narrow bays, rocky islands, Temagami outer channels**Common Descriptions:**

- looks like a log floating
- then turns
- then begins swimming
- then rises just enough to show hair or a head shape
- sometimes climbs onto shore on two or four limbs

Most sightings occur at dusk or moonlight, where the boundary between shadow and substance blurs.

Unique Pattern: Often approaches camps quietly, then vanishes into the water again.

7. THE NIGHT HOWLERS & SCREAMERS

(Vocal Entities / Unknown Mammalian Calls)

Common Regions: Nasmith Creek, Temagami River, White Bear Forest**Vocalizations Include:**

- deep chesty roars
- long, rising howls
- short barking blasts
- scream-like human sounds

Not wolves.Not foxes.Not owls.Several rangers and biologists have confirmed the calls don't match known species.

Unique Pattern: Animals go silent *before* the howls begin.

8. THE CAMP DISAPPEARANCE PHANTOMS

(Entities Associated with Missing Campers)

Common Regions: Smoothwater, Cross Lake, remote islands**Behaviors / Clues:**

- perfect circular disturbances around tents
- camps fully intact yet abandoned
- fires still warm
- no tracks
- equipment untouched
- sudden silences before disappearance

These cases suggest a form of **lure** or **silent approach**.No visible creature, but the pattern is consistent and chilling.

Unique Pattern: Circular disturbance rings, often 1–3 meters from tents, are found in multiple cases across decades.

BEHAVIORAL PATTERNS ACROSS TYPES

Despite their differences, several startling similarities repeat across many entity types.

Pattern 1 — Silent Approach

Most creatures or entities approach camps without:

- footfall noise
- brush movement
- snapping twigs
- water splashes
- breathing sounds (until very close)

This silent arrival is one of Temagami's most unnerving traits.

Pattern 2 — Circular Movement

Circling a structure, tent, or clearing appears repeatedly:

- Bigfoot-type entities
- Whisperers
- Disappearance cases
- Ridge Shadows

Circling may be:

- territorial
- investigative
- ritualistic
- a warning

It is not random.

Pattern 3 — Night Preference

Nearly all encounters occur:

- after midnight
- before sunrise
- during windless, silent conditions

Many witnesses report the air feeling "charged" before events.

Pattern 4 — High Curiosity, Low Aggression

In most cases, entities:

- observe
- circle

- knock
- manipulate objects
- slap walls
- breathe beside tents

but rarely attack.

This suggests intelligence and intention — not instinctive predation.

Pattern 5 — Avoidance of Light

Flashlights, spotlights, and lanterns often result in:

- sudden silence
- retreat
- vanishing
- circling farther away

Entities prefer darkness to observe without being seen.

Pattern 6 — Seasonal Shifts

Some entities appear more in certain seasons:

- **Bigfoot-like forms:** spring–fall
- **Ridge Shadows:** summer–early fall

- **Whisperers:** mid-to-late summer
- **Aquatic forms:** mid-summer, low-wind conditions
- **Disappearances:** late summer–fall
- **Howlers:** spring–late fall

Winter sightings are rare but often far more dramatic.

Pattern 7 — Silence Before Appearance

Animals stop:

- moving
- calling
- feeding

Moments before encounters.

This "dead-silence phenomenon" is one of the strongest shared signs across all types.

CONCLUSION — TEMAGAMI'S UNKNOWN ECOLOGY

This appendix isn't a list of monsters.It isn't a catalogue of folklore creatures.It's a field-based look at the **repeatable patterns** emerging from decades of independent encounters.

If you strip away names, cultural interpretations, and assumptions, you're left with:

- tall forest entities
- sub-surface aquatic shapes
- whispering and mimicking voices
- silent nighttime prowlers
- ridge silhouettes
- auditory anomalies
- disappearance-linked disturbances

These may represent:

- different species
- different manifestations of a single phenomenon
- unknown natural forces
- or something else entirely

Temagami doesn't provide answers. It provides patterns.

And the patterns tell us one thing for certain:

There is more living in this wilderness than we currently understand.

APPENDIX E — ANOMALIES FOUND IN THE TEMAGAMI WILDERNESS

Physical Evidence, Environmental Oddities & Unexplained Patterns

Temagami is filled with stories — but every once in a while, the wilderness gives something solid. Something physical. Something you can touch, photograph, measure, or feel beneath your boots.

These anomalies don't prove anything. But they challenge everything.

Below is a categorized list of **real-world anomalies** repeatedly found across Temagami's forests, lakes, islands, and portages — the kind that make even experienced researchers pause.

1. STRUCTURAL ANOMALIES

1A — Tree Breaks Too High for Humans or Bears

Height: **7 to 10 feet above ground**Break type:

- twisted, not snapped
- fibers spiraled
- intact bark
- pointed downward, not outward

Appears frequently near:

- White Bear Forest
- Nasmith Creek
- Lady Evelyn backcountry

Why it's an anomaly: Wind breaks tear outward. Snow load bends downward. Bears break branches lower.

These breaks show intentional twisting force.

1B — Leaning Trees Forming "Frames" and "Bows"

Common Sites:

- Wolf Lake trails
- Obabika old growth
- Temagami River corridor

These structures involve:

- multiple trees woven together
- trunks bent into arches
- large logs placed at precise angles

Possible explanations:

- Bigfoot-type structures
- winter storm stress

- old trail-marking methods (less likely)

Field notes: Many of these structures occur far from trails, deep in inaccessible regions.

1C — Stone Stacks & Tapping Stones

Found on:

- small rocky islands
- remote portages
- ridgeline clearings

Features:

- stones balanced in impossible configurations
- stacks appearing overnight
- tapping sounds heard at night

Anomaly: No boot prints or animal tracks near them, even in soft moss or spring mud.

2. FOOTPRINT & TRACK ANOMALIES

2A — Single Tracks With No Approach or Exit

Seen most often in:

- moss beds
- shallow mud
- island shorelines

Characteristics:

- one perfectly formed footprint
- deep impressions
- no prints leading toward it
- no prints leading away

Sometimes the print sits in the center of undisturbed forest floor.

Interpretation: Suggests a vertical arrival or departure — or something stepping only once.

2B — Track Lines Ending Abruptly

Common in:

- snow
- sandy shorelines
- leaf litter

Rules broken:

- no stride change

- no disturbance
- final print often deeper than others

In winter: Perfect tracks ending in untouched powder.

2C — Massive Handprints on Canoes & Rocks

Seen on:

- aluminum canoes
- dock surfaces
- smooth granite slabs

Features:

- wide spread
- long finger-like impressions
- print always wet even with dry weather

Often found **in the morning**, suggesting nocturnal activity.

3. ACOUSTIC & ENVIRONMENTAL ANOMALIES

3A — Sudden Global Silence (Complete Stop of All Wildlife)

Usually precedes:

- shadow figures
- footsteps around tents
- water disturbances
- disappearances

Duration: 15–90 seconds (or longer during disappearance-linked events)

Anomaly: Silence includes:

- no wind
- no insects
- no birds
- no water movement
- no branch motion

It is as if the world "switches off."

3B — Directionless Voices

Not whispers — full voices.

Types:

- distant conversation
- one clear word

- mimicry of familiar voices

Location:

- Wolf Lake region
- Obabika Old Growth
- Cross Lake portages

What makes it anomalous: Voices don't travel properly; echo comes from wrong direction or nowhere at all.

3C — Low-Frequency Ground Vibrations

Often reported near:

- Maple Mountain
- Temagami River at night
- Obabika basin

Witnesses describe:

- faint humming
- ground pulsing
- chest vibration

Measurable? Sometimes yes — felt through canoe hulls or cabin floors.

Cause remains unknown.

4. AQUATIC ANOMALIES

4A — Underwater Pulses Against Canoe Hulls

Witnessed on:

- Lake Temagami
- Obabika Lake
- Diamond Lake trenches

Feels like:

- a slow heartbeat
- a deep underwater thud
- a pressure wave

Frequency:Often appears in patterns (3 pulses, pause, repeat)

4B — Sub-Surface Shadows Larger Than Canoes

Consistent traits:

- smooth movement
- no fin or tail

- long ellipsoid shape
- glides silently

Appears in:

- dead-calms
- glassy water
- moonlit nights

Not sturgeon.Not logs.Not boats.

4C — Perfect Circular Swirls in Calm Water

Appears around stationary canoes.

Diameter:1–3 metersCenter:Deep downward pull or bubble line

Often follows canoe movement.Disappears in shallow water.

5. CAMP & CABIN ANOMALIES

5A — Disturbance Circles Around Tents

Diameter:1–3 metersDepth:Pressed into pine needles, moss, or soil

Found in:

- disappearance cases

- cabin pacing events
- whispering zone camps

Significance: Indicates repeated circling by a heavy entity.

5B — Cabin Slaps With No Prints

Impact force: Strong enough to shake walls Yet:

- no bear scratches
- no muddy prints
- no tracks in soil

Often accompanied by heavy breathing or soft exhalation.

5C — Rocks Placed on Tent Roofs

Sometimes small pebbles. Sometimes fist-sized. Found at:

- island camps
- peninsula camps
- remote backcountry lakes

Usually placed gently, not thrown.

Anomaly: No tracks outside tent.

6. LIGHT & ATMOSPHERIC ANOMALIES

6A — Low-Flying Orbs & Ground-Level Lights

Colours:

- blue
- white
- amber

Behaviors:

- hovering
- weaving between trees
- following shorelines
- rising vertically and vanishing

Seen in:

- Wolf Lake
- Obabika Old Growth
- Lady Evelyn corridor

6B — Starfield Distortion ("Stars Going Out")

Witnesses report:

- patches of sky suddenly black
- stars blinking out for seconds
- shadows moving under starlight without wind

Often accompanied by nausea or vertigo.

6C — Column of Fog Appearing From Nowhere

A vertical cylinder of mist forming on clear nights. Location-specific:

- Maple Mountain base
- Obabika lowlands

Inside the fog:

- footsteps heard
- whispers
- cold air

Disappears in seconds.

7. ANIMAL BEHAVIOR ANOMALIES

7A — Loons Diving and Not Emerging Where Expected

Loons normally surface within predictable ranges.In some hotspots:

- loons dive
- reappear 50–80 meters away
- or vanish entirely during disturbances

Possible predator avoidance?Unknown.

7B — Moose Leaving Lakes in Sudden Panic

Several lakes show:

- moose entering the water
- suddenly turning
- sprinting out as if fleeing something beneath them

Often correlates with sub-surface shadow reports.

7C — Wolves Shadowing Camps Without Making a Sound

Not aggressive — curious. But unnatural lack of vocalization.

Often precedes whisperer-type anomalies.

8. PSYCHOLOGICAL & PERCEPTUAL ANOMALIES

8A — Time Gaps / Lost Minutes

Witnesses describe:

- noticing the fire burned much lower than expected
- thinking only seconds passed
- but finding 20–40 minutes gone

Most often during:

- whisper events
- footsteps around camp
- deep night calm

8B — Sudden Emotional Overwhelm

Feelings of:

- dread
- sadness

- euphoria
- disorientation

Often in specific areas, like:

- Obabika big pines
- Smoothwater valleys

Not typical fear. Something deeper.

8C — "Being Watched" Sensation That Stops Instantly

This sensation ends sharply, as if a switch was flipped.

Often followed by:

- silence
- a snap of a branch
- or footsteps moving away

CONCLUSION — THE PATTERNS BEHIND THE IMPOSSIBLE

These anomalies don't form a single narrative. They form a mosaic —pieces scattered across decades of reports, left behind like breadcrumbs from something unseen.

You can dismiss stories.You can deny creatures.But anomalies?

They're physical.Measurable.Recorded.Photographed.Repeated.

And they suggest one thing:

Temagami isn't just haunted by stories — it is shaped by something alive, ancient, and still watching.

APPENDIX F — INDIGENOUS QUOTES & INTERPRETATIONS ON THE MYSTERIES OF TEMAGAMI

Respectful Reflections from the Anishinaabe Worldview

Temagami lies within the traditional lands of the Teme-Augama Anishnabai — the Deep Water People. Their relationship with this region is ancient, layered, and deeply spiritual. While many traditional teachings are private, there are well-known public statements, cultural beliefs, and widely shared interpretations that offer profound insight into the mysteries described in this book.

This appendix gathers **commonly cited Indigenous quotes** and **broad interpretations**, honoring the voices who have lived with this land far longer than any modern researcher.

1. "Everything in the forest has a spirit, even the things that look still."

Interpretation:

In Anishinaabe worldview, the land is alive. Trees, rocks, lakes, and animals carry spirit and intention. The idea that "stillness" means "nothing is there" is a European misunderstanding.

In Temagami, this explains why:

- silence often precedes encounters
- certain lakes are avoided

- some islands are never camped on
- animals behave strangely in specific places

The land may be responding to something unseen.

2. "There are places where you do not shout."

Interpretation:

Some regions of the backcountry are considered "heavy places." They're not evil — they are **sacred**, or **inhabited**, or simply places where spirits are active.

These warnings align with:

- disappearance hotspots
- whisper-zone portages
- lakes with sudden fog columns
- areas where sound dies unnaturally

To shout or behave aggressively is believed to disturb the spirit of that place.

3. "The little people are not small in power."

(A reference to the Memegwesi — widely known in Anishinaabe stories)

Interpretation:

The Memegwesi are often described as:

- small beings
- living near water, cliffs, or caves
- shy
- curious
- easily startled
- occasionally mischievous
- quick to react to disrespect

They are said to be protectors of certain places.

Temagami has many such spots:

- cliff bases
- river narrows
- rock outcrops
- ancient pine roots

Strange noises, small footprints, tapping, or rock tossing may align with these older stories.

4. "If you feel watched, you probably are."

Interpretation:

This saying relates to the belief that **spirits observe visitors**, especially at night or near sites of significance.

It resonates strongly with:

- ridge watchers
- shoreline silhouettes
- unseen eyes from treelines
- the overwhelming "being watched" sensation

This interpretation isn't sinister —it simply means one is not alone, and the land is aware of you.

5. "Do not camp where the wind won't go."

Interpretation:

Areas where air feels heavy, still, or "wrong" are often avoided. This aligns with:

- dead-silence phenomenon
- fog pillars

- emotional overwhelm
- sudden dread

Indigenous teachings suggest such places are **not for people**, regardless of what causes the feeling.

6. "Some lakes hold old stories at the bottom."

Interpretation:

Deep lakes, especially ones with sheer drop-offs, are often considered "mysterious" — not in a horror sense, but because they have **depth in both water and spirit**.

This aligns with:

- sub-surface shadows
- underwater pulses
- canoe bumps
- moose panicking
- lights rising from water

The teaching implies the water is alive with memory.

7. "Watch the animals. They know before we do."

Interpretation:

Animals are seen as messengers.Their behavior signals what is happening spiritually or physically.

Examples in Temagami:

- wolves going silent
- loons diving and not resurfacing normally
- moose fleeing deep water
- birds avoiding certain islands

These reactions may reflect predators, spirits, or natural forces — but the principle remains:

Animals sense the unseen.

8. "The land chooses who it shows itself to."

Interpretation:

Not everyone will experience something unusual.Not everyone is meant to.

This aligns with your experience:years of Temagami research, and the sense that encounters happen when the wilderness allows them.

It reframes the mystery:

The land is not hiding.It is selective.

9. "Respect is the first tool you pack."

Interpretation:

In every Indigenous teaching, respect is the foundation of safe travel. Respect for the land, spirits, animals, and unseen forces.

Those who camp carelessly often have frightening or unsettling experiences.

Those who move with humility tend to be left alone — or visited gently.

10. "The spirits of the forest do not shout. They whisper."

Interpretation:

This is often said in reference to:

- whispers
- calling of names
- soft laughter
- distant conversation

These are not seen as ghosts, but as **the forest speaking**.

Not dangerous — but not to be ignored.

11. "Do not mock what you do not understand."

Interpretation:

Mocking or challenging spirits is believed to invite trouble. This applies to:

- yelling into the woods
- taunting whatever made a sound
- confronting unseen footsteps
- assuming dominance

Many disappearance stories across the north begin with disrespect.

12. "There are beings who walk upright that are not us."

Interpretation:

This quote appears in many different Anishinaabe communities, and is one of the oldest references to **tall forest beings**.

Not evil. Not demons. But **older-than-human forest people** who avoid contact.

The idea is not far from modern Bigfoot encounters — but the interpretation is less about biology and more about **coexistence**.

CONCLUSION — A WAY OF SEEING, NOT A SET OF ANSWERS

These Indigenous teachings don't "solve" the mysteries of Temagami. They don't classify creatures or spirits or anomalies.

Instead, they offer a **framework of respect**, a way to see the forest as:

- alive
- aware
- layered
- meaningful

And they remind us that Temagami's mysteries are not new.

They are older than the maps, older than the cabins, older than the trails, older than the stories in this book.

The land has always been speaking.

Indigenous people have simply been listening longer than the rest of us.

APPENDIX G — FIELD SAFETY & SURVIVAL GUIDELINES

Practical Advice for Campers, Paddlers, and Researchers Working in Mysterious or High-Strangeness Zones

Temagami is one of the most beautiful, rugged, and spiritually charged wilderness regions in North America. It is also, as this book has shown, a place where the ordinary rules of the woods don't always apply.

Most trips into Temagami are safe and uneventful.But when unusual activity does occur — whether it's mimicry, watchers, cloaked figures, silence events, or boundary crossings — campers and researchers must have a clear safety protocol.

This appendix outlines **field-tested, realistic safety guidelines**, blending wilderness experience with the emerging patterns documented throughout this book.

These guidelines are meant to help you:

- stay calm
- stay grounded
- stay aware
- stay safe
- recognize when it's time to back out

And most importantly:**know what not to do.**

This is not fearmongering — it is preparation.

1. GENERAL WILDERNESS SAFETY (FOUNDATION)

These rules apply before anything unusual even happens.

Whether you're researching cryptids, photographing nature, or simply camping, the basics are non-negotiable:

Tell someone your exact route and return time.

Do this even if you've traveled the area many times.

Carry more water and food than you think you need.

Unexpected events — natural or otherwise — can delay travel.

Pack proper navigation tools:

- paper topo maps
- compass
- backup compass
- GPS with extra batteries

Prepare for sudden weather changes.

Temagami can shift from calm to dangerous in minutes.

Carry a PLB or satellite communicator.

Starlink, Garmin inReach, or Zoleo — something that works off-grid.

Never assume cell service.

You won't have it.

Set up camp before dark whenever possible.

These basics save lives long before the unusual ever enters the picture.

2. SAFETY WHEN YOU FEEL WATCHED

The earliest and most common sign that something is observing you.

Many people panic the first time they feel "watched" in Temagami.But the watchers rarely approach and almost never behave aggressively.

What to do:

- Stay calm.
- Keep speaking normally to your partner(s) if you aren't alone.
- Make no sudden movements toward the forest.

- Maintain natural noise (humming, talking softly, rustling gear).

- Keep your campfire going — watchers rarely cross firelight.

- Do not shine lights directly into the treeline. (This escalates tension.)

- Stick together if you're with a group.

What NOT to do:

- Never chase a watcher.

- Never attempt to flank it.

- Never yell at it.

- Never throw objects into the forest "to scare it off."

Watchers observe from a distance. Treat them like wildlife with intelligence — not like intruders.

3. SAFETY DURING MIMICRY EVENTS

Voices calling your name, footsteps matching yours, cries from the shoreline.

Mimicry is psychologically dangerous because it targets instinct — not logic.

If you hear your name called:

- Freeze and listen, but do not approach the sound.
- Confirm your partner's position if you're not alone.
- Speak only to people you *can see*.
- Retreat toward open space or water.

If you hear a child crying:

Do NOT investigate it alone. This is one of the most dangerous lures.

If you hear someone who sounds like your friend:

Call back to your real friend — if they answer from another direction, leave immediately.

If footsteps mimic your own:

- Stop walking.
- Wait.
- Turn your body slowly in a full circle — but do not step toward the sound.
- Retreat calmly toward camp.

Golden Rule:

If you can't see the source of the voice, you do not respond to it.

4. SAFETY IN DESOLATE ZONES

Total silence, nausea, pressure changes, emotional flattening.

These areas are among the most dangerous in Temagami because they signal a boundary shift.

If silence falls suddenly:

- Stop moving.
- Speak quietly to ground yourself.
- Note your surroundings.
- Slowly leave the area in the same direction you entered.

If you feel dizziness or chest pressure:

This is a known boundary symptom — exit immediately.

If animals refuse to enter:

DO NOT force your way in. Animals know these zones better than humans.

If your compass spins:

Leave. Do not attempt to "power through."

5. SAFETY WHEN ENCOUNTERING GIANTS OR LARGE SILHOUETTES

Giants are not aggressive — but they are territorial and purposeful.

If you see one at a distance:

- Remain still.
- Do not shout.
- Do not lift binoculars (this can appear predatory).
- Slowly back away while facing the being.
- Maintain calm breathing.

If it remains stationary while watching you:

You are likely near a boundary.Respect that.Change your route.

If it steps sideways or shifts position:

This is a warning.Retreat immediately.

6. SAFETY ON THE WATER (LAKE CREATURE ZONES)

Deep trenches, strange currents, silent risings.

These guidelines apply when encountering underwater anomalies:

If a massive shadow rises under your canoe:

- Stay centered.
- Do NOT lean over the gunwales.
- Do NOT tap the canoe or slap the water.
- Paddle calmly to shallower water.

If your canoe is followed:

- Maintain course.
- Avoid sudden direction changes.
- Do not stop over deep trenches.
- Head to the nearest shoreline.

Never swim at night in deep-basin lakes.

Ever.

7. SAFETY DURING SKY LIGHT OR AERIAL ANOMALIES

If you witness lights moving above the treeline or over lakes:

Do:

- Observe from cover.

- Turn off bright flashlights.
- Document quietly if possible.
- Move away from open water.

Do NOT:

- Paddle directly beneath lights
- Attempt to signal them
- Flash bright lights upward
- Follow their direction of travel

Lights often hover above the boundary interior — stay out of that region.

8. SAFETY WHEN THE FOREST "REARRANGES"

If you wake to moved objects, altered trails, or reset camps:

Stay calm.

Panic wastes energy and leads to bad decisions.

Perform a quick check:

- Gear accounted for
- Food untouched or altered

- Tracks around camp
- Any missing time

If multiple objects have moved:

Leave the area that morning. This is environmental-level interaction.

If your trail vanishes or redirects:

Never follow a trail that "wasn't there yesterday." Retrace your steps instead.

9. RED FLAGS THAT MEAN YOU SHOULD LEAVE IMMEDIATELY

These conditions signal a threshold you are not meant to cross:

- sudden boundary silence
- mimicry targeting your name
- cloaked figures seen twice or more
- repetitive giant sightings in the same direction
- deep underwater hums growing louder
- fog that moves against the wind
- multiple desolate-zone symptoms at once
- your dog refusing to continue

- GPS malfunction + emotional heaviness
- footsteps matching your own rhythm
- camp rearrangements combined with mimicry

If any TWO of these occur in combination, **you leave. Immediately. No debate.**

10. MENTAL SAFETY — THE PART TOO MANY IGNORE

Psychological safety is crucial.

You are not the exception.

No amount of experience removes the risk of panic or disorientation.

Debrief after every unusual event.

Talk openly about what was felt and observed — suppressing fear increases mistakes.

Recognize environmental deception.

Some phenomena manipulate perception — sound direction, emotion, memory.

If someone in your group panics:

- Stay close

- Speak calmly
- Keep them walking
- Do NOT split up under any circumstance

If you feel drawn deeper:

This is a documented effect of mimicry and boundary proximity.Stop.Turn back.

Your instincts are not wrong in Temagami.They are working overtime to keep you alive.

11. FINAL GUIDELINE — WHEN IN DOUBT, LEAVE

This rule has saved more lives than any survival technique:

If something feels wrong,you turn around.Immediately.No ego.No bravado.No exceptions.

Temagami rewards respect.It punishes arrogance.

And the intelligence described throughout this bookresponds not to force,but to boundaries.

APPENDIX G - TOP 10 MOST DISTURBING TEMAGAMI ENCOUNTERS

The Most Unsettling, Unexplained Events Ever Recorded in the Temagami Wilderness

These ten cases represent the **most chilling, behaviorally unusual**, and **consistently corroborated** encounters in the Temagami region. Some involve vocalizations or pacing; others involve mimicry, physical contact with structures, or whole camps going silent. What unites them is a single theme:

Whatever is out there behaves with a level of awareness that does not fit known wildlife.

1. The 2009 Temagami Cabin Photographs (The "Cabin Watcher")

A couple staying at a remote cabin captured **three photographs** of a massive upright figure between cedar trees. Minutes earlier, they heard **two-note whistles** from different directions, followed by **slow bipedal pacing** and the cabin door shifting on its frame. They fled the next morning and never returned. This remains one of Ontario's most compelling visual cases.

Disturbing Because: The creature approached a human dwelling, displayed communication signals, and did not flee when photographed.

2. The West Temagami Hunting Family Encounters (2017–Present)

Over several seasons, a hunting family has experienced:

- Long stride tracks
- Pacing in total darkness
- Mimicry of voices
- Whistles and wood knocks
- Figures watching from treelines
- A massive shape approaching their camp at dawn

Each year, the pattern intensifies slightly.

Disturbing Because: The phenomenon appears **territorial** and **repeat-patterned**, suggesting intelligence and area familiarity.

3. The Rabbit Lake Cabin Siege (2010)

Veteran hunters endured two nights of **growls, screams, pacing, and violent slaps** against their cabin walls. Something large circled repeatedly at close range and hit the building with tremendous force. They abandoned the trip after no sleep for 48 hours.

Disturbing Because: The creature demonstrated physical strength, persistence, and an almost taunting awareness of the cabin occupants.

4. The Whispering Portage (1989)

Two brothers heard their **names whispered** from the trees while walking a portage at night. No lights, no footsteps, no animals. The whispers grew closer, then fell silent all at once.

Disturbing Because: Accurate mimicry of human speech is one of the rarest and most unsettling behavioral patterns in these phenomena.

5. The Night Visitor Slap Case (2024)

In Central Temagami, a backcountry cabin was struck **three separate times** about twenty minutes apart. Witnesses reported a **soft, chest-deep sighing** outside afterward — too low and resonant to be human.

Disturbing Because: The slow, deliberate timing suggests intention, not reactive behavior.

6. The Lake Temagami Growl & Scream Audio Event (2011)

A family recorded loud, deep growling followed by **piercing screams** echoing across the lake at night. Interviews confirmed the vocalizations were unlike wolves, moose, or bears.

Disturbing Because: The sound carried power and tonal clarity far beyond known wildlife.

7. The Maple Mountain Ridge Walker Photograph (2011)

Hikers photographed a **tall, narrow silhouette** walking along a distant skyline ridge. No tracks were found. The figure moved with unnatural smoothness and vanished from view without descending either side.

Disturbing Because: The subject moved in a controlled, upright manner that does not match human hikers.

8. The Island Rock Footsteps (2018)

Clear bipedal footsteps were recorded on bare granite late at night. The sound was heavy, rhythmic, and close. At dawn, **no prints** were found on the rock.

Disturbing Because: The clarity of the footsteps versus the total lack of physical sign is a pattern often reported in high-strangeness cases.

9. The Shadow-Cliff Traverse (2022)

Witnesses saw a **tall shadow** cross a sheer cliff face at a distance — moving smoothly, without climbing motions, and without dislodging stones.

Disturbing Because: The movement defied physical explanation on the terrain.

10. The Sharp Rock Canoe Scrape (2023)

Two paddlers felt a **massive underwater body** scrape slowly along the underside of their canoe at night. The scrape was deep enough to vibrate the hull. No fish or known animal in the region matches the behavior or scale.

Disturbing Because: The deliberate contact implies awareness, size, and proximity — all in the darkness below.

BONUS: 2025 Whisperer-Uptick Summer (Multiple Lakes)

Several unrelated groups reported **hearing their names called** from the shoreline or woods. Same cadence. Same tone. Same impossible direction of travel.

Disturbing Because: This pattern is usually isolated; an uptick across lakes suggests a regional behavioral spike.

APPENDIX I — ACTIVE HOTSPOTS INDEX

Current Areas of Elevated Activity in the Temagami Wilderness

This index highlights the regions within and around Temagami where recent reports, field investigations, audio captures, and multi-year encounter patterns indicate **heightened levels of unusual activity**. These hotspots are based on a combination of witness statements, long-term researcher observations, wildlife reactions, consistency of behavior, and geographic clustering.

1. West Temagami — Multi-Year Encounter Corridor

Status: Active since 2017**Primary Activity:**

- Tree knocks
- Whistles
- Long-stride tracks
- Figure sightings
- Seasonal return patterns

This remains Ontario Bigfoot's most consistent long-term study zone, with repeat seasonal encounters reported by the same hunting family.

2. Rabbit Lake Sector — Vocalization & Pacing Zone

Status: Active (2010, 2014, 2023 echoes)**Primary Activity:**

- Screams
- Growls
- Heavy pacing around structures
- Cabin slaps
- Multi-directional calls

The 2010 "Cabin Siege" remains one of the most aggressive nighttime encounters in Temagami's modern history.

3. Obabika Old Growth — Whisper Phenomena Region

Status: Intermittent**Primary Activity:**

- Whispering voices
- Whistle triangulation
- Silent-drop forest behavior
- Possible mimicry patterns

This ancient cedar forest has produced some of the region's most unsettling auditory anomalies.

4. Diamond Lake Basin — Underwater Shadow Zone

Status: Consistent patterns (1979, 2006, 2020)**Primary Activity:**

- Pressure waves
- Subsurface tracking
- Moose panic reactions
- Mist-column events

Evidence suggests something large or multiple somethings patrol this basin in near-total silence.

5. Maple Mountain Ridge & East Approach

Status: Ongoing**Primary Activity:**

- Ridge walker sightings
- Silhouettes on skyline
- Odd movement patterns
- Long-range observation behavior

Maple Mountain is one of the most spiritually and geographically significant sites in Temagami — and one of its most mysterious.

6. Sharp Rock Channel System

Status: Active **Primary Activity:**

- Canoe scrape events
- Drifting lights
- Unexplained water disturbances
- Cabin taps & mimic-knocks

Sharp Rock is a recurring hotspot for **both** water-based anomalies and shoreline pacing events.

7. Central Temagami Cabin Belt

Status: Recent increase (2024) **Primary Activity:**

- Night slaps
- Deep sigh vocalizations
- Slow approach behavior

Cabins in this cluster have reported repeated nighttime contact with unseen visitors.

8. Lady Evelyn High Ridge & Cliff Traverse

Status: Active (2022–present) **Primary Activity:**

- Tall silhouettes
- Cliff-edge traversal
- Large-mass movement in steep terrain

Witnesses have described unnaturally smooth movement across exposed faces.

9. Gull Lake Crown Land Sector

Status: Expanded interest**Primary Activity:**

- Rock impacts
- Close-range tree knocks
- Pacing outside firelight
- Low-frequency mumbling

A remote-access ridge and lakeshore zone where experienced field researchers have encountered multiple disturbing nighttime events.

10. Wolf Lake & Cross Lake Corridor

Status: Historically active**Primary Activity:**

- Voices behind campers
- Disappearances
- Night pacing
- Persistent isolation anomalies

- Sudden silence zones

This corridor has produced high-strangeness reports for nearly fifty years.

11. Temagami River Spine

Status: Recurring patterns**Primary Activity:**

- Deep, chesty howls
- Breath-against-tent encounters
- Distant pacing along banks

A mix of old encounters and modern incidents suggests a migratory or travel route.

Summary: The Patterns That Emerge

Across these hotspots, five behavioral patterns repeat:

1. **Triangulated whistles**
2. **Close-range pacing**
3. **Mimicry and vocal anomalies**
4. **Subsurface or shoreline movement**
5. **Tree knock signaling**

What makes Temagami remarkable isn't just the number of locations —it's the *consistency of the patterns* across decades, witnesses, and terrain.

These hotspots remain the most likely regions for future encounters, continued research, and field investigations.

ACKNOWLEDGEMENTS

Books like this are never written alone.They are built on shared miles, shared stories, shared nights around the fire, and the quiet understanding that the wilderness still holds more questions than answers.

First and foremost, I want to thank **the Temagami wilderness itself**.Every lake, ridge, cedar stand, and silent valley has shaped this book more than I ever could. Temagami has a way of humbling you, unsettling you, and filling you with a strange kind of reverence that lingers long after the trip is over. This land is not just a setting — it is a character, a teacher, and a guardian.

To the **field researchers**, past and present —the ones who spent long nights listening, long days tracking, and long hours studying patterns that don't fit neatly into maps or reports. Your work, often quiet and uncelebrated, forms the backbone of everything in these pages. Your respect for the land, your discipline, and your refusal to embellish or sensationalize are what keep this subject grounded.

To the **witnesses** who trusted me or a friend with their stories — thank you. Many of you shared memories you've carried for years, some for decades. You spoke honestly about fear, confusion, awe, and the moments that changed the way you see the forest forever. This book exists because you were brave enough to speak.

To my fellow paddlers and partners on the trail —those who stuck by me through fog, rain, broken gear, strange nights, and the unforgettable feeling of something pacing just out of sight. You know who you are. Your presence made the wilderness feel a little less vast on the dark nights.

To the **Indigenous Elders and knowledge-keepers** who shared warnings, stories, and teachings about the land — miigwech. Your insights changed how I approached Temagami and helped me understand the difference between curiosity and disrespect. Without your guidance, this book would lack its most important layer of truth.

To my friends and family who have always supported my strange mix of fieldwork, research, and late-night writing sessions — thank you for understanding the pull this work has on me, and for never telling me to "just write something normal." Your encouragement kept this project alive when the pages grew heavy.

Finally, to every reader who has ever stepped into the northern wilderness with an open mind —thank you. Temagami does not reveal its secrets easily. If this book has made you pause, look a little longer at the treeline, or feel the presence of something older than the land itself, then these chapters have done their job.

There is wonder here.There is danger.There is mystery.And there is beauty.

Thank you for walking this trail with me.

www.ingramcontent.com/pod-product-compliance
Lightning Source LLC
Chambersburg PA
CBHW071958150426
43194CB00008B/924